Making Lemonade

S0-AQL-777

Making Lemonade

What others are saying about Making Lemonade...

"The benefits of a positive perspective are obvious, for happiness, success, relationships, and even health. Less obvious is how one can become more positive, and MAKING LEMONADE contains dozens of suggestions playfully packaged in accessible recipes. Readers are urged to try out those that make most sense. All you might lose is your pessimism."
-Christopher Peterson, Professor of Psychology, Director, Michigan Positive Psychology Center, University of Michigan

"Here's a recipe for you: Take a full bowl of scientific evidence, add plenty of common sense to make it digestible, and then mix it with lemonade to sweeten it even more. What you get is this delicious book that can provide bite-size advice for all those interested in savoring life."
-Tal Ben-Shahar, Best-selling author, Happier and In Pursuit of Perfect

"Making Lemonade contains a breathtaking array of immediately useful and inspiring information on how to turn negatives into positives. Dr. Farber's latest book is relevant to everyone as it can be used to turn around a life or fine-tune a problem area! Each of the 101 recipes is a no-frills and directly-to-the-point description of a positive trait or perspective and what exactly you need to do to achieve it. This book can be read from cover to cover or skimmed like a book of recipes. What aspect of your life would you like to improve today? The step by step recipe is probably in this book."
-Dr. Peter Bandettini, Ph.D. Chief, Section on Functional Imaging Methods, Director, Functional MRI Core Facility, National Institute of Mental Health.

With a sly sense of humor and a kind heart, Dr. Farber has given us "food" for the soul. In brief and entertaining snippets, readers are encouraged to think about established values, attributes and axioms in new ways. His insights are often the product of behavioral science research, while the suggestions feel as comfortable and wise as those dispensed by a trusted family member. This is a delightful book that is funny and touching, but more importantly could positively impact the reader in a profound and potentially life-changing way.

-Afton L. Hassett, PsyD, Associate Research Scientist, Department of Anesthesiology, Chronic Pain & Fatigue Research Center, University of Michigan Medical School

"Dr. Farber has written a recipe book that should find its way into every home. Making Lemonade is packed full of healthful strategies, steps and formulas to living a happier life. The recipes are practical, satisfying, and are sure to make you smile. This is a most nourishing path to empowerment! A great way to start off your day with a fresh perspective."

-Anita Stangl, President & Chief Executive Officer, Alliance for Smiles – Medical Missions for Children

This book is lemonade for the soul. Dr. Farber's strategies and tips are simple, practical, fun and refreshing.

-John Gordon, Best-selling author, The Energy Bus and Soup

"The latest scientific data crunched down into delicious bite sized recipes that all readers can enjoy and use. I really liked this book!"

-Sarah Pressman, PhD, Assistant Professor of Psychology, University of Kansas.

"Dr. Farber's latest work is packed full of practical recipes for personal empowerment, general well being, and happiness. It provides the reader with almost instant refreshment for the daily challenges of the human condition. Its simplicity and organization make it a nourishing reference for regular use as we encounter the myriad of opportunities provided to us in daily life. I would highly recommend this book to anyone looking to quench the thirst created by the human psyche. I suspect that after the first use it will become a treasured guide and a top gift giving choice for family, friends, and colleagues."
-Mark S. Gridley, MBA, Vice President Physician Affairs FHN Healthcare

"Dr. Farber has contributed significantly to the literature on transforming environments, organizational cultures and attitudes through development of positive approaches to problems we all face. Making Lemonade is an engaging approach that allows any reader to break down common struggles and define a positive approach. I have "tried" many of the recipes from the book and "cooking" with this on my reading list has definitely improved my overall health."
-Dr. Joseph Kerschner, Dean and Executive Vice President, Medical College of Wisconsin Professor, Department of Otolaryngology and Communication Sciences Medical College of Wisconsin

Making Lemonade

101 Recipes to Convert
Negatives into Positives

Neil E. Farber M.D., Ph.D.

DYNAMIC PUBLISHING GROUP
MEQUON, WI

Copyright ©2012 by Neil E. Farber, M.D., Ph.D.

Published by Dynamic Publishing Group, Mequon, Wisconsin

All rights reserved. No part of this publication may be reproduced, stored in a retrieval system, or transmitted, in any form or by any means, electronic, mechanical, photocopying, recording or otherwise, without the prior written permission of the author.

Limit of Liability/Disclaimer of Warranty: While the publisher and author have used their best efforts in preparing this book, they make no representations or warranties with respect to the accuracy or completeness of the contents of this book and specifically disclaim any implied warranties of merchantability or fitness for a particular purpose. The advice and strategies contained herein may not be suitable for your situation. You should consult with a professional where appropriate. Neither the publisher nor author shall be liable for any loss of profit or any other commercial damages, including but not limited to special, incidental, consequential, or other damages.

Front and Back Cover Design by Matteo Garcia

ISBN – 978-0-9853024-2-9
LCCN - 2012934686

Printed in the United States of America

Other books by Dr. Farber

The Blame Game. The Complete Guide to Blaming: How to Play and How to Quit. Bascom Hill Publishing, MN, 2010.

The No Blaming Zone: An allegorically true story about creating positive changes, harnessing energy and achieving your potential through the simple act of taking responsibility. Dynamic Publishing Group, WI, 2012.

The Financial Industry's Guide to the No Blaming Zone, Dynamic Publishing Group, WI, 2012.

Please check out Dr. Farber's Blame Game Blog on www.PsychologyToday.com.

Contents

Recipes

Converting Negatives into Positives

Staples: Basic dietary items to wet your positive palate. Inexpensive with plenty of energy, protein and dietary fiber.

Appetizers: Starters, lighter fare, easier to accomplish

Soups and Salads: Mixed bag of positive products

Entrees: Main courses, heartier, better quality and pay-off

Desserts: Delectable finishes completing your meal and satisfying your optimistic appetite for something sweet.

Dedication

With love I dedicate this book to my eldest daughter Kaelah Rachel. Kaelah, who is currently living in Israel, is a free spirit and an independent soul. Your positive attitude is my inspiration and an eternal source of wow. You are an expert at turning bad into good.. You are strong and well balanced physically and emotionally with an infectious sense of well-being, an extraordinary ability to see goodness in all situations, and a resilience that puts Teflon to shame.

Acknowledgements

This book would never have been written if not for the positive influence of my mother, Linda. Luckily for me, she is a fabulous cook who has collected several hundred recipe books. While I was looking for a new way to express old thoughts, the idea of a recipe book suddenly became apparent and obvious. This book was a labor of love and there are many people to thank for making it a reality.

Thank you to my children, Kaelah, Shoshana, and Sarena. You are amazing; strong-minded individuals with kind hearts and loving spirits. I hope that this book helps you continue on your positive journeys to wherever your paths lead. I know you will all flourish.

Thank you to my parents, Linda and Michael (OBM) who, throughout my life, have contributed to this book. Your recipes for happiness are inspirational and invaluable.

I give credit to my positivity teachers throughout the years, even though some of whom don't realize that I have been a dedicated and indebted student: Drs. Stephen Covey, Ellen Langer, Tal Ben-Shahar, Martin Seligman, Barbara Fredrickson, Sonja Lyubomirsky, Mihaly Csikszentmihalyi, Dan Gilbert, Christopher Peterson, and Deepak Chopra. Tal Ben-Shahar, you have been a fabulous "go to" guy when I come up with ideas and want to see if they make sense. The seeds that you have planted have sprouted, flourished and made their way to paper. Thank you.

A special thanks to my friends Jon Gordon, author of the Energy Bus and The No Complaining Rule and David Pollay, author of The Law of The Garbage Truck. You have both encouraged me to look for a new format to get my message out and are great sources of inspiration. I would like to recognize the support and knowledge passed onto me by the following spiritual leaders: David Cooper and Marc Berkson.

Much gratitude is due to members of the Wellness Task Force of the American Society of Anesthesiologists as well as the Positive Health division of the International Positive Psychology Association and their leaders; Drs. Robert Holzman, Gail Randel, Martin Seligman, Antonella Delle Fave, and Afton Hassett. You have all been a great source of support.

My mentors in anesthesiology, who have supported and encouraged my non-traditional pathway in medicine. Dr. John Kampine, Dr. David Warltier and Dr. George Hoffman – you have facilitated bringing positive psychology into our practice and our hospitals. Thank You.

I would be remiss if I did not thank my clients who allow me to work with such wonderful people in your organizations. Thank you to all of my students, my patients, and my coworkers. I am appreciative that you allow me into your lives and help me so much more than you could ever realize.

Introduction

"Always turn a negative situation into a positive situation.
~ Michael Jordan

The truth is that I was not always hugely fond of lemons – straight up anyway. Sure, like most people, I'd squeeze a lemon over my fish or into a glass of water for some flavoring, but for me, biting directly into a lemon was rather sour. I know that the sour feeling did not just stay in my head, it was well-broadcast by a puckered and furrowed look on my face. My daughter, Shoshana on the other hand loves lemons. I really admired how she could take a big bite of a lemon and smile just like she was biting into a sweet fruit; sometimes I wondered if we were really eating the same food – so sour for me, so sweet (it appeared) for her. I thought that it was a fact that lemons were *supposed* to be sour. "I'm a scientist" I told my daughter, "lemon juice is about 5% to 6% citric acid with a pH of 2 to 3; that makes them sour." She would just take another bite and smile.

My feelings about lemonade are different. At the mention of lemonade, do you think of Florida's Best® or Snapple® Brand? Perhaps you have a preference for Mike's Hard Lemonade®. I like them all. I love lemonade! Plain lemonade, flavored lemonades and even the fancy designer lemonades are great with any meal. When I think of lemonade, I also think of Dale

Carnegie's famous quote, "When fate hands you a lemon, make lemonade."

Carnegie was born in 1888 and like his famous quote, made the transition from a poor farmer's boy to the successful developer of popular courses in self-improvement, salesmanship and interpersonal skills. He is well known for his 1937 bestselling book, *"How to Win Friends and Influence People."* Not only could he teach; Dale Carnegie could also do. He was one of the world's most successful men in addition to being a grandfather of the self improvement movement. His lemon quote hit home for me. For many years I had been a big proponent of trying to focus on positive things. Creating something good - "lemonade" from something bad - "lemons" made sense to me and I began to "make lemonade" using several of the recipes in this book.

So, you're asking, is this just another book that talks about positivity in terms of lemonade? Just like you, I hope not. There are many excellent books available by extremely talented authors, teachers and researchers on the specific benefits of positivity, optimism and happiness and the problems and consequences of negativity and pessimism. I can't improve on what's been said by Drs. Daniel Gilbert, Barbara Fredrickson, Christopher Peterson, Tal Ben Shahar, Jonathan Haidt, Sonja Lyubomirsky, Martin Seligman, Ed Diener, Ellen Langer, and Mihaly Csikszentmihalyi to name a few. These are the true experts on the subject and I have learned much from them. They have conclusively demonstrated that positive, optimistic, happy people are mentally, physically and emotionally healthier; they have an enhanced immune system, are more resilient, have better relationships, are more successful at work and in marriage, are more satisfied with their lives and careers, and even live longer!

Why are there so many positivity books? Because there is so much negativity in our society and we need help. Every day, everywhere I go, and almost everyone that I interact with has a diet consisting predominantly of lemons. Like most people, I would frequently use the word "lemons" as a replacement for the word "bad". Yet, I kept thinking about how Shoshana would bite into a lemon and taste something good. Sure, like many people, she loves lemonade, but she also loves lemons. She found something redeemable, worthwhile, and good in the lemon itself. Since she was about two years old, she would bite into lemons and smile like she was eating a sweet fruit. In essence, Shoshana mindfully makes lemonade when she bites into a lemon. Did the lemon become lemonade while sitting in her mouth? While many of the recipes in this book are useful to convert apparent negatives into positives and "make lemonade", Shoshana also taught me to look closely at what most people reflexively believe to be negative and perhaps see something positive.

In this way, Carnegie's quote isn't complete. Don't assume that lemons are bad. It is not the lemon that is bad or good, but how we positively or negatively react to or interpret an event, situation, or thing (the lemon) that leads to our happiness or discontent.

Let's take a closer look at lemons. The lemon is actually a small evergreen tree as well as the yellow fruit of the tree and it is used for culinary (juice, pulp, and rind) and non-culinary purposes throughout the world. (As an incidental note, the lemon rind is known as zest and the word zest is one of the character strengths associated with positivity.) The lemon probably first grew in India, Myanmar and China. In Asia, it was known for its antiseptic properties and it was used as an antidote to treat poisons.

What else do we know about lemons? Following are some of the uses and benefits of lemon juice of which you may or may not be aware: get rid of stubborn ink spots, brighten fingernails, clean and disinfect your cutting board, brighten your white clothes as a bleach substitute, treat a nose bleed, take the sting out of insect bites, stop insects from coming into your home, treat eczema (mixed with olive oil), refresh and relieve dry skin, clear blackheads and pimples, lighten age spots, lighten freckles, treat a sore throat (with honey and olive oil), remove berry or beet stains, prevent dandruff, create hair highlights, treat athlete's foot (mix with Papaya juice), disinfect and sanitize the garbage disposal, bring out the shine in your utensils and stainless steel cookware, clean and deodorize your microwave, polish chrome faucets, stop sliced apples and pears from discoloring, keeps your guacamole looking fresh, prevent rice from sticking, freshen soggy lettuce, remove rust and mildew stains, relieves poison ivy itch, help relieve constipation, removes fish odors, remove warts and sooth sunburns.

While I am not recommending any of the following as effective treatments, here are some more purported uses of lemons: redden your lips (practiced in the court of Louis XIV), relieve discomfort from arthritis, act as an anti-inflammatory agent, enhance relaxation, treat insomnia, help alleviate coughs, treat hoarseness, treat urinary retention, stimulate appetite, aid digestion, treat scurvy, and decrease ringing in the ears (tinnitus). Lemons are also a great source of vitamin C which enhances the immune system to keep you healthier. Incidentally, lemons can also be used to help clean a food grater, decorate and cheer up a room, and prevent fish from sticking to a grill. Lemons contain lots of important ingredients: dietary fiber, protein, iron, potassium, magnesium, calcium, zinc and the antioxidants, bioflavonoids; in addition to most of the B vitamins.

Keep in mind that we have all of these reported benefits of lemons in the absence of (so far) any significant side effects. Now can you look at this huge list of rewards and advantages and think of anything other than lemons are a fabulous fruit? They are really amazing! Does it make you want to put down this book, go and get some lemons? If so, resist the urge for a while, I'd like you to finish this chapter. We have all had experiences where we hear of a word or phrase with which we weren't previously familiar; and now that word appears often and in many different contexts. This is now the case with me and lemons.

Since I started writing this book, I see the words lemons and lemonades in so many things that I look at. Last night when I turned on the television there was an infomercial discussing the health and weight loss benefits of a "lemonade diet". This morning I drove by a restaurant with an advertisement for "minionade", some kind of fruit-based, ultra-sweet lemonade, inspired by the animated movie, Despicable Me.

Things, events and situations may seem bad to us because of a lack of information, misinformation, pre-existing biases or closed-mindedness. When we pre-define things as bad, we start from a negative position and have to work harder to find something positive. If you label everything that doesn't make you happy as "bad":

- You rely on external things and events to make you happy.

- You rely on other people to make you happy.

- You become an energy vampire.

- You hinder the development of productive relationships.

- You lose control and responsibility over your life.

- You believe that situations, not you, create good and bad.

- You develop self-helplessness.

- You incur physical, emotional, spiritual and psychological consequences of negativity.

Redefine Bad

"If you realized how powerful your thoughts are, you would never think a negative thought." ～ Peace Pilgrim

The first important recipe to change an apparent negative into a positive is to try to redefine "bad". Instead of trying to make something good out of it, perhaps it is already good, but we just don't appreciate that yet. This concept has been incorporated into several of the recipes throughout the book (such as #7, 8, 12, 15, 19, 37, 41, 45, 50, 56, 57, 63, 64, 72, 80, 88, 92, 94 and 96). Realize that the negative labels that we apply are subjective and based on our perceptions; not on the intrinsic nature of the thing or person or event being evaluated. So what can you do to make these into positives, First, don't try to fake it. Don't just say, "OK fine, it's all good", if you don't feel it. You will be even more frustrated if you smile and put up with what you consider badness. Studies have shown that a fake (Pan-American) smile is as much a predictor of myocardial ischemia or lack of blood flow to the heart as negative emotions such as anger.

Try not to compare people, things or events to the past, the future or some fictitious gold standard. Reflect on your life's plan to live well, be happy and be positive. This will set the right mood to help you redefine to the positive. The realization that it is in your own best interest to redefine "bad" as "good", will enhance your intrinsic motivation! Prepare yourself psychologically to reinterpret events in a positive way. Enjoy the present. Enjoy the moment. Relying on memories or dreams won't make you happier; they prevent you from truly enjoying each experience.

Appreciate that things happen for a reason and the reason isn't always readily apparent. If you believe this, you will be able to sustain a more positive outlook. Look for "blessings in disguise". There is usually a door that opens when one closes. Even those events that initially appear to be absolutely bad, and beyond the possibility of being good or beneficial or positive, may not be so in certain situations or under certain conditions or within certain cultures.

I was once hit in the eye by a weapon and incurred a deep corneal laceration and double vision out of that eye. Upon hearing this, I wouldn't be surprised if you thought this was a "bad" event. However, the ophthalmologist that I saw about the injury was also able to diagnose that I had glaucoma. Further testing revealed that I had already lost some peripheral vision in both eyes. I was immediately started on treatment and was thus spared any further significant losses. Thank God I was hit in the eye otherwise I would have lost more vision. For me it was a "good" event.

After a minor car accident, my hands started tingling and slowly became weakened. I was diagnosed with spinal cord impingement and required a cervical neck fusion. "Bad" event right? Well, it turned out that much of the narrowing in my spinal canal was pre-existing (although I never knew about it) and the doctors informed me that I was really lucky to have had such a minor incident push me over the edge. If I had taken a hard fall during one of my martial arts classes, jumping on the trampoline, or off the diving board, I could have easily become quadriplegic. Another "good" event – a blessing in disguise.

Blessings in disguise are everywhere and if you assume that there is one, you will have a better chance finding it. Even if you are one hundred percent sure in your belief that another person or thing is to blame, you might still be wrong; you can never be 100% sure. We rely on our senses but they are not always correct.

This book is not about relying on positive affirmations to make you feel better or about wishing yourself happier. This book is also not about putting on a happy face and faking it; getting lemons and pretending that you are satisfied with the lemon juice or just trying to make the best of a bad situation. That will only take you so far. Most of the recipes in this book will give you practical and useful ways to change how you act or react or alter what you do in order to convert "bad" things to "good" things and thereby bring more positivity into your life. Other recipes will focus more on ways to redefine what you think is bad. For years, I have taught many of the recipes and techniques in this book to satisfied students, clients and patients with excellent results.

The book is divided into food categories with several recipes for each category. Like many recipe books, each item includes: what we have (*The lemon* – apparent negative), what's required (*Ingredients* – what we need to make a conversion), what we'll do (*Preparation* – how to make a conversion) and what we'll get when we're done (*Lemonade* – the positive result).

All of the recipes and techniques that I have listed have some basis in research and experimental data. A few of these recipes have been handed down to me from my parents and grandparents, others were taught to me by school educators, martial arts instructor, meditation guides, mindfulness teachers, and spiritual/religious leaders. Some recipes I just picked up along my life journey, heard about from friends, or read about in other recipe books. As a scientist and researcher I recognize the importance of evidence-based information rather than what is often presented by self-help gurus as "this seems like it would work". A recipe that works with one person has all of the statistical significance of a miracle.

Very few of these recipes do I claim to have invented or discovered although I often have included my own version of the recipe to enhance the flavor or alter the seasoning. Throughout the book I try to give credit to the creator of a recipe if I know the source. Like following any cookbook, the recipes may seem to be more difficult than they first appear. Converting negatives to positives is indeed hard work; it takes concentration, effort, and time, although I always find it worthwhile. And like any other skill, the more you practice, the easier they get. Most of the recipes in this book are relatively fast and easy to accomplish and somewhat more difficult to master. Just as in traditional recipe books, where you might let something simmer on the stove or cool down for ten minutes, allow some time (approximately ten to fifteen minutes) with many of these recipes, for thoughtful self-reflection, relaxation or meditation. On average, most of the recipes described in this book can be completed from start to finish within thirty minutes to one hour.

If you read a recipe that just does not speak to you, skip over it and move onto something that resonates with you. Individual tastes differ. Perhaps on a second reading of the book, that same recipe that you couldn't get yourself to read, will reach out to you and perhaps even become one of your favorites. This same philosophy also applies to redefining bad. As I'm writing these words, I'm sucking on a lemon – and smiling!

If you have more lemonade recipes that have worked well for you and you don't mind sharing, please send them to me at neil@dhwi.net to be included in the next Lemonade book, which is in progress.

Neil E. Farber, M.D., PhD.

Making Lemonade

STAPLES

1. Take responsibility: don't play the blame game

"A man can get discouraged many times but he is not a failure until he begins to blame somebody else and stops trying." ~John Burroughs

• *The Lemon:* Being angry, frustrated or disappointed because you think something bad has been done to you. Reflexively blaming others or events and shifting responsibility away from yourself. Blaming often helps you feel better in the short term, but in the long term, you lose control of your life. Blaming inhibits our ability to achieve successful relationships, careers, and personal growth.

• *Ingredients:* <u>Knowledge</u> - that no one controls you – except you. <u>Responsibility</u> – an essential ingredient! <u>Honesty</u> – with yourself. <u>Confidence</u> – that you are able to be accountable. <u>Self-control</u> – don't jump to conclusions. <u>Respect</u> – believe that others are not always out to get you. <u>Faith</u> and <u>Hope</u> – that things will work out for the best.

• *Preparation:* Know that you may not be able to control everything that goes on outside of you, but you have this uncanny ability to control what goes on inside of you. Since you are in total control of your feelings, words, actions, and responses – you are accountable and responsible. Be honest with yourself when you feel like someone or something else is at fault. Acknowledge that had those same people or events apparently caused you to achieve greatness, they may not have been credited with your success. Mix in a healthy amount of confidence to accept the responsibility no matter the outcome. This confidence will also be a positively attractive character trait to others. Use your self-control to not assume and jump to conclusions when you rush to blame others. Begin with a basic respect for other people whether you know them or not. Don't assume that they are out to get you. Don't assume that the universe is out to get you. Don't ever ask, "Why me?" (Unless you just can't believe how lucky you are). Blend your faith about things working out for the best with your hope for a bright future and you will start thanking rather than blaming others.

• *The Lemonade:* Once you accept responsibility for your thoughts, feelings, and actions; once you stop blaming others for things that you can actually control, you will be empowered to achieve your greatest potential. Your stress levels will decrease. You will strengthen all of your relationships. You will improve your job satisfaction and chances for a successful career. You will feel better about other people and find yourself in a more relaxed and peaceful state.

2. *Respect*

"Respect your efforts, respect yourself. Self-respect leads to self-discipline. When you have both firmly under your belt, that's real power." ~Clint Eastwood

"This is the final test of a gentleman: his respect for those who can be of no possible service to him"
~William Lyon Phelps

• *The Lemon:* Lack of self-respect. Disrespect and disdain for other's feelings and for others' beliefs. It doesn't get much more sour than this. Leaves you with a very strong acerbic taste in your mouth. It leaves other people with the sense that you have a superiority complex – not a healthy characteristic.

• *Ingredients:* Open-mindedness – not prejudging. Fairness – a healthy dose of equality. Justice – having a sense of honesty and integrity to be even-handed. Teamwork – cooperative work ethic. Compassion – a pinch of compassion can go a long way. Love – for you and others.

• *Preparation:* Guess where it starts? With you. Focus time: 1 minute to look in the mirror and make sure that you respect the person looking back at you. This is easier when you are living according to your own principles and values. Start with an open mind when you meet someone new or even better yet, when you encounter someone with whom you've had negative dealings. Begin by giving everyone the benefit of the doubt. Try not to judge people by what they wear or how they look. If you give them a chance, their story may surprise and even inspire you. Try to be fair to others by treating them with integrity and justice. Realize that everyone not only has potential, but they also have many positive qualities. Sometimes they take a little while to find – but that doesn't make them less worthwhile. Try to develop beyond just tolerating others to the point of considering the health and productivity benefits of teamwork. Finally move beyond getting along well together, to the point of feeling compassion, caring, and empathy towards others. At the end of this road to respectful positivity is the feeling of love toward our fellow (wo)man. Keep in mind that everyone has had their personal challenges and issues with which they have dealt and this deserves our respect.

• *The Lemonade:* When you finish preparing this lemonade, you'll be left with the feeling that everyone is valuable and has purpose. Obviously, productive relationships must be built on feelings of mutual respect. Respect forms the basis for flourishing and successful marriages, corporations, and careers – a very sweet lemonade indeed!

3.   Practice forgiveness

"When you hold resentment toward another, you are bound to that person or condition by an emotional link that is stronger than steel. Forgiveness is the only way to dissolve that link and get free." ⁓Catherine Ponder

"Forgiveness is both a decision and a real change in emotional experience. That change in emotion is related to better mental and physical health."
⁓Everett L. Worthington, Jr. PhD

"Forgiveness is the fragrance that the violet sheds on the heel that has crushed it." ⁓Mark Twain

• *The Lemon:* You skipped recipe #1 and played a round of blaming. Now you've not only given up control and responsibility, but you have decreased your chances of developing close interpersonal relationships. When you continue to harbor feelings of blame, this resentment will inhibit your empathy, trust, altruism, and compassion; not just toward the blamee, but toward others as well.

• *Ingredients:* Focus on Now – get over the past. Emotional strength – forgiveness represents strength, not weakness. Kindness – treat people with goodwill. Fairness – being open-minded. Empathy – understanding other peoples' viewpoints. Altruism – you'll need a spirit of generosity to help others.

• *Preparation:* Forgiveness involves the ability to move beyond the past and focus on the present and the future. Ruminating and dwelling on hurts, limits your ability to enjoy the now and plan for a productive future. Don't confuse forgiveness with approval or with weakness. Forgiving someone allows you to put the past where it belongs; it does not condone wrong behavior. You can't make this lemonade without the ability to treat people with kindness, fairness, and empathy. The Golden Rule: do unto others...isn't just for Sunday school classes. One of the greatest forms of altruism is the gift of forgiveness. As with other forms of giving, when you forgive, you'll experience a "helpers' high" and you'll be helping yourself as well. While there are many, Drs. Everett Worthington and Robert Enright are two of the most prominent forgiveness researchers and proponents on forgiveness.

• *The Lemonade:* Benefits of forgiving are not simply applied to the target of blame. The primary benefits actually apply to the forgiver. Interestingly, unconditional forgiveness is associated with even greater well-being than forgiving those who offered apologies. Forgiveness has been shown to improve mood, reduce anger and anxiety, alleviate depression, and enhance life satisfaction. There are even unexpected benefits such as greater cardiovascular health and fewer physical symptoms. Yes, forgiveness is the path to inner health and healing. Talk about strong lemonade!

4. Commit

"The achievement of your goal is assured the moment you commit yourself to it." ~Mack R. Douglas

"Find something that you're really interested in doing in your life. Pursue it, set goals, and commit yourself to excellence. Do the best you can." ~Chris Evert

• *The Lemon:* Not being committed, attached, or actively engaged to something or someone. This may reflect disinterest, a lack of perseverance or self-discipline, poor interpersonal skills, or perhaps depression.

• *Ingredients:* Hope and Optimism – positive beliefs for the future and positive self-talk. Passion – With both your heart and your mind. Determination – strength of mind and resolve. Perseverance – persistence through challenges. Resilience - the capacity to cope with stress. Focus – concentration on the task at hand. Loyalty – essential strength. Conscientiousness – thoroughness. Courage – everyday heroism. Curiosity – at least a teaspoon.

• *Preparation:* It is impossible to be truly committed to something or someone without having positive, hopeful beliefs about what you expect to happen and without being passionate about what you are doing. Passion involves a raw determination to pursue a goal or course of action or relationship with hope and optimism. Adding persistence and perseverance, allows you to continue that commitment despite challenges. Being resilient allows you to cognitively change stressors and adversities into positive motivators. Being faithful, dedicated and devoted to an ideal or a task or a relationship always requires focus, loyalty, and conscientiousness. In addition, we are more likely to give up our quest in the face of confrontations. Thus, don't start mixing this lemonade if you don't have the courage to face those obstacles and the curiosity about what the next step will bring.

• *The Lemonade:* Being committed requires similar strengths to being goal-oriented. Bring achievement, determination, courage, and self-motivation to the table. These are positive character traits that are associated with success in all walks of life. Having or developing the ability to be persistent in the face of hardships and being loyal to a meaningful cause will also elevate your mood, enhance resilience, and improve your self-respect. Being committed will bring more meaning to your life and give you a renewed sense of purpose that will be evident to everyone around you. You will be an example to others and inspire greatness.

5. *Immerse*

"Caretake this moment. Immerse yourself in its particulars. Respond to this person, this challenge, this deed. Quit evasions. Stop giving yourself needless trouble. It is time to really live; to fully inhabit the situation you haZppen to be in now." ~ Epictetus

• *The Lemon:* Lack of attachment and dedication to a task is the pathway to failure. We fail to fully enjoy events in which we are not immersed. When we are engaged in a project but not fully aware, present, or immersed mentally, we waste time. We miss amazing opportunities for learning, growing, and pleasure. We can never achieve true potential or attain maximum pleasure when we are not mindful, aware, and immersed in what we are presently doing.

• *Ingredients:* Mindfulness – here and now. Passion – performing with zeal. Determination – strength of mind. Focus – concentration on the task at hand. Conscientiousness – thoroughness. Curiosity – what if...

• *Preparation:* It requires a smooth blend of mindfulness - active awareness of your thoughts, actions, and environment, with true fervor, excitement and enthusiasm for what you are doing. In truth, mindfulness by itself is non-judgmental. Exc*itement is ac*hieved by your "here and now" awareness. In psychology, we refer to the art of savoring – becoming mindfully engaged to heighten the effect of positive events on positive thoughts and feelings. Mindfulness is performed without judgment whereas savoring is mindfulness with a positively attitude. To this we add some determination and focus, which fortifies us to pursue our desires in the face of hardships and challenges without becoming distracted. When you are conscientiousness about this lemonade, you will find more enjoyment in a process that involves precision and care. Finally, topping it off with curiosity can add purpose to your involvement, as you maintain interest about where this journey of immersion will lead. Try to avoid immersing yourself in negative, unhealthy, or addictive habits. Realize that you can fully immerse yourself in many activities at the time that you are doing them while still maintaining balance in your life.

- *The Lemonade:* It is virtually impossible not to enjoy an activity or event in which we are fully immersed. Immersing yourself in anything (positive) will enhance your outlook and your optimism. Immersing yourself in conversations will enhance your relationships. Immersing yourself in work, will enhance your career success and job satisfaction.

6. Seek serenity

"Right thoughts produce right actions and right actions produce work which will be a material reflection for others to see of the serenity at the center of it all."

~Robert M. Pirsig

"But I do know focusing on the exterior doesn't make me happy. If I want peace and serenity, it won't be reached by getting thinner or fatter." ~Elle Macpherson

• *The Lemon:* Havoc and chaos are not conducive to peaceful, calm and healthy relaxation and thoughtful self-reflection. As a multitude of thoughts accumulate, we tend to ruminate on what we believe to be significant issues. Our minds get cluttered as we start to get dragged backwards into the past. This often leads to a spiral of negativity.

• *Ingredients:* A private location – somewhere comfortable. Time – minutes, not hours. Mental white out – to clear your calendar. Relaxation – a healthy serving. Focus – this time it is a focus on nothingness. Creativity – serenity is not always where you think it might be.

• *Preparation:* Find a nice quiet, private location where you can dedicate some time to be alone. You don't need a lot of time to find serenity – even 15 minutes may be enough if you have the aptitude. Before you enter into the "serenity space", make sure that you mentally clear your calendar. You can seek serenity, but have a difficult time achieving it if you are distracted and not focused specifically on decompressing and relaxing. You can't do this in front of the TV! Try a warm bath, sitting on the back porch, listening to soothing or spiritual music, lighting a candle, etc. For most of us, serenity does not come easily. Try to either focus on (1) your breathing, (2) perform a body scan; sequential relaxation technique progressing from your toes to your nose, (3) some creatively visualized perfect relaxing vacation. The challenge: random thoughts will continuously enter our minds. Do not give them energy by actively trying to get rid of them. Acknowledge that they are there and gently regain your focus. You'll need creativity to find the time to remove yourself from a busy schedule and then to find a great location. A few tablespoons of creativity will also go a long way toward taking you to a relaxing serenity space.

• *The Lemonade:* There are a multitude of mental, emotional, and physical health benefits from this serenity lemonade. At first, finding the time, place, and ability to relax may seem to be a daunting task. However, with little practice, you will be able to relax almost anywhere and at almost any time. You will be a sea of serenity amidst a storm of chaos. Simply the awareness of this achievement will quench your thirst.

7. Laugh

"You grow up the day you have your first real laugh -- at yourself."
~Ethel Barrymore

"I live to laugh, and I laugh to live."
~Milton Berle

"Good humor is a tonic for mind and body. It is the best antidote for anxiety and depression. It is a business asset. It attracts and keeps friends. It lightens human burdens. It is the direct route to serenity and contentment."
~Grenville Kleiser

• *The Lemon:* The belief that challenges and situations are all "problems". The inability to look at the lighter side of life. Negativity and sadness replace wit and humor. Frustration rules!

• *Ingredients:* Appreciation – a little positive reception for whatever comes your way. Hope – the best will come to pass. Flexibility – seeing things in a new perspective. Creativity – we all have some. Confidence – in yourself. An audience – you don't need to sell tickets.

• *Preparation:* Start with a sincere appreciation for all that life has to offer and the hope that things will get even better. Now realize that when we are stressed, frustrated, unsatisfied, and unhappy, there may be other ways of looking at the same situations. Step out from a single-minded perspective and see things from a different angle. Pouring in flexibility to reframe apparent negatives in a more positive way, will improve your resilience. Creativity will also help you to find humor in places that you would be surprised to find any – but it will be there if you look with an open-mind. When you miss your plane or you wait in line at the grocery store for forty-five minutes; yes, these can be maddening – or they can be funny. Look for reasons that you will laugh at this in the future; then don't wait! Start now and you'll feel so much better. Don't be limited to laughing at others. Have the confidence to also laugh at yourself. You don't need an audience, but the social reward for contributing to group laughter is exhilarating, uplifting, and empowering. A few friends can be a perfect audience. Remember, laugh with them, not at them!

• *The Lemonade:* Laughter has many physical and emotional beneficial effects. Humor helps us bond with others and improve our social connections. Humor helps us attain and maintain flexibility while viewing potentially challenging situations with a healthier, positive perspective. Laughter can help us recover from extreme distress. Is it all in your head? Perhaps, laughter elevates the brain chemicals endorphins (pain-reducing and mood-elevating) and dopamine (feel-good) and lowers the stress-related hormones, cortisol, and spigot. Research has also shown that the lemonade of laughter will also provide your immune system a hefty boost.

Neil E. Farber, M.D., PhD.

8. *Explain – don't complain*

"If you have time to whine and complain about something then you have the time to do something about it." ∼Anthony J. D'Angelo

• *The Lemon:* Complaining is toxic and mindless; damaging to relationships, marriages, careers and corporations. It initiates a widening spiral of negativity that quickly engulfs all who are unfortunate enough to stand in its path.

• *Ingredients:* Emotional intelligence – recognize and manage emotions. Reason – critically and logically. Communication – positively. Self-discipline, self-control, and moderation. Fairness – respect others. Focus – what can you change? Praise and Gratitude – opens our hearts to look for reasons.

• *Preparation:* Keep in mind high costs of mindless complaining and how easy it is to get sucked into being a participant once it starts. Avoid this trap by using your emotional intelligence to understand other people's emotions and to manage yours by not getting involved. Productive and positive changes almost never occur when we mindlessly complain. Substitute this negative behavior with positive communication styles. Use self-restraint and self-control to resist the temptation! Mindless complaining is damaging to relationships and not fair to others. Don't settle for things that are worthy of change, but focus on what is within your control to try to change and then use your communication skills and other persuasive talents to try to make it happen. As John Gordon, the author of "The No Complaining Rule" has described, justified complaining involves identifying a problem and moving toward a solution. Bring the issue to the person or people who can actually effect a change. John Gordon suggests some other anti-complaining methods such as The But ⟶ Positive Technique. When you start complaining, add the word *but* and then convert the rest of the sentence into a positive statement. Example: "I don't like my job *but* I'm glad that I've got one and that my family can afford to go on vacations." Another Gordon method is to convert "Have to" into "Get to". This is the road to positivity showing gratitude and praise. Realize that many of the things that you classify as "having to do" are actually things that you choose to do – including going to work. Make sure that you contribute potential solutions every time you identify an apparent problem.

• *The Lemonade*: "Turn justified complaints into positive solutions." John Gordon. Replacing complaining with positive forms of communication will empower your relationships, your business, and your life. You will have more energy and more stamina. You'll be able to take deeper breaths and have a greater satisfaction with those around you and life in general.

9. Cultivate and appreciate relationships

"People are lonely because they build walls instead of bridges." ~Joseph F. Newton

"Whenever you're in conflict with someone, there is one factor that can make the difference between damaging your relationship and deepening it. That factor is attitude." ~William James

• *The Lemon:* Loneliness. Conflict. Lack of a social support network. Being socially isolated. Boredom. Dumping your personal garbage on others (as David Pollay would say).

• *Ingredients:* Oxytocin - pituitary hormone, Moral support – who doesn't need this? A shoulder – nice and lean. Approachability – tend and befriend. Open-mindedness – always a good thing. Flexibility – mentally, not physically. Doubt – there's benefit in this. Leniency – seems pretty good to me. Gratitude – thanks for the memories. Social organizations – it's bigger than just you. *The Law of The Garbage Truck* - by David Pollay.

• *Preparation:* We are social animals. Chronic threats stimulate oxytocin release and a "tend and befriend" response. We join forces, share duties, and look out for one another. We widen our social circles and search for creative solutions. Cultivating close friendships involve a give and take of moral support and an occasional shoulder to cry on. Initiating friendships requires trust, curiosity, eye contact, and proper body language and attitude. This says to prospective friends, "Hi, I'm approachable." Friendships turn sour if they are not seen through the eyes of being open-mindedness and flexible. When you get frustrated with someone, realize that you may not know the whole story. Don't jump to conclusions even if they seem logical. Your opinion is subjective. Friendship doesn't just lead to more positivity; optimists are better at making friends. They're also better at giving people the benefit of the doubt and classifying events and characteristics as being positive. That alone is worth a big "Thank You". Get permission to vent your anger or frustration. Appreciating relationships, involves avoiding dumping your garbage on others and helping others not dump their garbage onto you.

• *The Lemonade:* Happiness that comes from social networking is contagious and easily spread. If you're a social person, you probably have a boosted immune system with more antibodies to fight infections. Close relationships enrich our lives by increasing our life satisfaction as well as our sense of security. To maintain friendships requires the use of much interpersonal strength, which in turn, develop when you value close friendships. Each relationship that you develop and value, adds fuel to this positivity cycle. Friendships also provide us with the external support needed to help us have a more positive perspective and the internal resilience needed to buffer against apparent obstacles. Friendships and groups also give us a better sense of confidence, hope, and purpose.

10. Relax

"Your mind will answer most questions if you learn to relax and wait for the answer." ~ William S. Burroughs

"The time to relax is when you don't have time for it." ~ Sydney J. Harris

• *The Lemon:* Things aren't going your way. You're late for an important appointment. That package hasn't come yet... You're up-tight, frustrated, anxious, disappointed, sad, or mad. Lemons!

• *Ingredients:* Wisdom – to know the difference. Deep breath (perhaps several). Determination: make it happen. Open-minded and flexible – seems we need these a lot. Hope – optimistic spirit. Creativity – oh, the possibilities. Inanimate Objects – something that induces a relaxation response.

• *Preparation:* You're stressed out. Can you do anything about it? Do you have the ability to change what's going on? If the answer is "yes", then stop being anxious, angry, frustrated, and sad. Relax and do something about it! You'll have a much better chance of success if you take a deep breath and focus your energy on accomplishing change than if you waste your energy on fruitless, simulated lemonade. Becoming goal-directed to effect change will also help you to relax with a renewed sense of purpose and self-determination. Now, if the answer is "no", you can't do anything about what is frustrating or stressing you out, than Relax. How will worrying help? It will certainly hurt you physically, mentally, socially, and emotionally. It will be a waste of time and energy; a waste of vital human resources and a needless stress on your support network. In the end, it won't change the outcome and you will be more upset. Rather, be open-minded, flexible, and hopeful to the possibility that what has happened may be for a greater good that you don't yet understand. Be creative with coming up with possibilities of how this may benefit you or others. Recruit some inanimate objects to help such as a relaxing book, soothing music, a candle, a peaceful walk. Relaxation is your first step toward meditation; a practice which is chock-full of health and wellness benefits.

• *The Lemonade:* Relaxation enhances contentment. It brings about a sense of mindfulness and allows us to appreciate just being. Relaxation is not simply a passive exercise. Relaxation is considered an active mood management skill to improve your emotional intelligence; your ability to not just notice but to understand subtle emotional cues that arise from ourselves and others. This helps us form closer relationship bonds as well as more job and career satisfaction and performance.

11. Happiness comes from doing

"If you observe a really happy man you will find him building a boat, writing a symphony, educating his son, growing double dahlias in his garden. He will not be searching for happiness as if it were a collar button that has rolled under the radiator." ~ W. Beran Wolfe

• *The Lemon:* There is a poor correlation between having things like money, cars, and other inanimate objects with happiness. Happiness is not a destination or a place. We think that if we just get this particular thing it will make us happy – but shortly after we get the object of our desire, we are back to where we started – no happier. Do you want to win the jackpot? Would that make you happy? Jackpot lottery winners actually have an increased chance of losing friends, divorce, alcoholism, gambling, and only a transient improvement in happiness.

• *Ingredients:* Rest and exercise. A job – that is a calling. A hobby or leisure activity that you enjoy. A means to find flow. Friends and close relationships. Involvement in Religion or something Spiritual - Belief in something greater than yourself. Gratitude – true appreciation. Laughter – and a contagious sense of humor. Resilience – your bounce-back factor.

• *Preparation:* Happiness is related more to doing than having: being in healthy supportive relationships, positively engaged in work, involved in leisure activities, exercise, being optimistic, and having great social connections. Indeed it more often comes from within than from without. Finding flow occurs when you are totally engrossed in an activity. Time flies by quickly and being involved in the activity is its own reward. Happiness often comes from our relationships, including relationships with religious and social organizations. Happiness doesn't just come from attending religious services, there should be some greater spiritual beliefs involved - a belief in something greater than yourself. Often this is exhibited through altruistic behavior. In general, being appreciative and showing gratitude is highly associated with happiness. The ability to laugh and find humor in unpredictable situations coupled with the aptitude to relax and meditate to find serenity will always help you find that happy path. Our inability to cope with stress and adversity is a leading cause of unhappiness. We can develop resilience through Martin Seligman's PERMA - Positive emotions, becoming fully Engaged in activities, enhancing Relationships, finding Meaning in your life and appreciating our Accomplishments,

• *The Lemonade:* Happy people live longer. They have greater satisfaction with life, career, and marriage. Studies show that they are also more successful in their jobs and relationships. Happy people don't just complain less about their health; they are in fact healthier. Being happy is correlated with having more friends and a greater social support network. Happy people are more resilient, more attentive, and better at multi-tasking.

12. Be curious

"Everything is material for the seed of happiness, if you look into it with inquisitiveness and curiosity. The future is completely open, and we are writing it moment to moment. There always is the potential to create an environment of blame -- or one that is conducive to loving-kindness."   ~Pema Chodron

• *The Lemon:* Being apathetic, indifferent, and uninterested. This is the first step to being listless, lethargic, lazy and bored – tired, old lemons.

• *Ingredients:* Love of learning – the pursuit of knowledge. Eagerness – approaching the search with zest. Open-mindfulness – the ability to look at each situation with an unattached, non-judgmental attitude. Courage – valor and daring to find out something new. Fortitude – don't let apparent obstacles stop your journey of discovery.

• *Preparation:* Always something new to learn; something new to try to understand; something new to appreciate. Being curious does not mean "putting up with" new things or "willing to try" new things. It means an eagerness and desire to know, learn, and experience. Curiosity necessitates having an open-mind to what you might encounter and the courage, fortitude, and determination to pursue the answer in the face of adversity. In reality, the heightened awareness and excitement that is associated with the pursuit, acts as a buffer against potential obstacles.

• *The Lemonade:* Curiosity helps prevent boredom and apathy. Isidor Rabi, the Nobel laureate in physics was asked, "Why did you become a scientist, rather than a doctor or lawyer or businessman, like the other immigrant kids in your neighborhood?" His answer was "My mother made me a scientist without ever intending it. Every other Jewish mother in Brooklyn would ask her child after school: 'So? Did you learn anything today?' But not my mother. She always asked me a different question. 'Izzy,' she would say, 'did you ask a good question today?' Curiosity correlates with living a long life and curiously, it also correlates with better physical health. Curious people are more likely to investigate and explore issues and topics related to health and well-being. They are also the type of people to seek out hobbies and activities that produce flow – an optimally engaged state.

13. Be hopeful

"What oxygen is to the lungs, such is hope to the meaning of life." ~Emil Brunner

"Hope is not the conviction that something will turn out well but the certainty that something makes sense, regardless of how it turns out". ~Vaclav Havel

• *The Lemon:* Despair, hopelessness, despondency, anguish, misery and depression. Such a sad lemon. ☹

• *Ingredients:* Optimistic attitude – add this ingredient to everything. Goals – make them specific. Confidence – self-reliance. Enthusiasm and Motivation – not just being eager, but with passion.. Creativity – need this to conceptualize goals and pathways. Determination – don't give up. Resilience – this will be self-perpetuating once you develop some hope.

• *Preparation:* Hope entails an optimistic attitude and belief system. Be resourceful to investigate whether you can play an active role in having your hopes fulfilled. If you can contribute to the outcome and choose not to, you are engaging in wishful thinking. This may result in unrealized expectations and sour lemons. If you can take action, formulate your goals and delineate potential pathways to achieve them. Seriously and with focused awareness conceptualize the goals. Through this goal pursuit, excitement and enthusiasm will arise and in turn lead to more creativity and determination. Use these positive traits to help find ways to achieve these goals. Now blend in some motivation and reliance to complete the task and convert obstacles and problems into challenges. Be confident that good things will come to pass.

Hope may also entail a dream or wish that good things will happen to others. You may not have as much control over making these dreams come true but maintaining enthusiasm, motivation, and resilience will help you remain hopeful despite apparent obstacles that may arise. As the band Journey reminds us, "Don't Stop Believin'".

• *The Lemonade:* Hope is a transcendent strength which helps us face the future and any apparent obstacles and challenges with confidence and even enthusiasm. Hope is a critical factor for psychological health. It acts as a buffer to protect against negative emotions. Hopeful people are more focused on disease prevention and consequently, hopeful athletes are more successful in their performance and hopeful students in academic achievement.

Neil E. Farber, M.D., PhD.

14. Conquer fears

"The greatest barrier to success is the fear of failure."
~Sven Goran Eriksson

"FEAR is an acronym in the English language for "False Evidence Appearing Real." ~Neale Donald Walsch

- *The Lemon:* Doubts and fears are energy suckers. Once they are given any power they will quickly take over your life in a negative way. Fear-based decisions are limiting. They are stifling and life-draining. They discourage creativity, curiosity, hope, and courage. Having fears limits our social circle and our ability to seek out new hobbies, careers, activities, and relationships.

- *Ingredients:* <u>Determination</u> – to accomplish. <u>Motivation</u> – to experience. <u>Values</u> – variety to choose from. <u>Goals</u> - to achieve. <u>Purpose</u> – helpful in creating intrinsic motivation to pursue your goals. <u>Curiosity</u> – it may have killed the cat but it will help you go farther than you might otherwise. <u>Hope</u> – for something better or different.

- *Preparation:* Start with a combination of determination, to achieve something (anything that may be challenging) plus motivation to broaden your experiences. This is now the time to pour in some values in which to aspire and goals in which to achieve. The addition of the values and goals directed toward some well-defined purpose, allows one to pursue a dream despite hardships and apparent obstacles. When you top off the lemonade with curiosity about what it will be like when the goal is accomplished and hope that the future will be brighter and that your efforts will be worthwhile, any associated fears will become meaningless and slowly melt away.

• *The Lemonade:* When you have conquered fears – you're drinking a brave and courageous lemonade. To conquer fears requires resilience and determination. Similarly, the result of conquering fears is an increase in resilience and determination. Courage is one of the positive goal-oriented strengths that boost spirits and self-respect. Bravery is a trait that can help you become successful in any hobby, job or sport that you pursue. Courage may help you achieve great things by taking calculated risks and effecting positively inspiring changes in the world. Alternatively, small spoonfuls of daily courage, allow you to easily deal with everyday occurrences of what other people would consider hardships, challenges, or problems. Developing bravery allows you to broaden your horizons and experiences, become more extroverted, widen your social circles, deepen your emotional attachments, and increase your learning and life experiences.

15. Be open-minded

"And who can doubt that it will lead to the worst disorders when minds created free by God are compelled to submit slavishly to an outside will? When we are told to deny our senses and subject them to the will of others?" ～Galileo Galilei

• *The Lemon:* Narrow-minded, bigoted, prejudice, biased, and intolerant. When you are closed-minded, you pre-judge and don't give the benefit of the doubt. You hinder and injure all of your relationships. With a closed mind, you close yourself off to new ideas and thus cease to grow, develop achieve your potential. With this attitude, you will not be adventurous in relationships, hobbies, or careers. This results in less exploring and less new information gathering.

• *Ingredients:* Respect – for those around you. Doubt – could you be wrong? Curiosity – what else could it be? Courage – to change what you are comfortable with. Ambition – to create a better you. Aspiration – you have amazing potential.

• *Preparation:* Don't even start mixing ingredients unless you have some basic respect for others. That includes friends, foe, and strangers. To this respect, you then add a pinch of doubt. To achieve open-mindedness entails that you are confident in the fact that you don't know everything. Others may be right and we may not understand the whole story. So, while you are giving the benefit of the doubt to others, hold onto a little bit of self-doubt.

Be open to the possibility that you may have mis-judged, mis-heard, or mis-read. Now if you are curious about learning new things and meeting new people and have the courage to try to change from stale old negative habits, you can start to see some relationships improve and stress levels decrease. To complete the recipe, it helps to blend in some ambition about what you hope to achieve by becoming more flexible and the drive and sense of purpose to accomplish this task.

- *The Lemonade:* Being unbiased and tolerant. This will be readily apparent to all who interact with you. You will go through life with a lot less useless stress and anxiety over things that other people do. You will be much more relaxed and happy in the realization that things that used to bother you actually have no effect on anything that you do. In this low stress state you have also benefited from the additional knowledge that comes with flexibility. Now that you are not just willing, but excited about trying new things and meeting new people, you are learning and experiencing new things at record pace. This fills your life with awe and amazement – a truly fizzy lemonade!

16. Be compassionate

"If you want others to be happy, practice compassion. If you want to be happy, practice compassion."

~Dalai Lama

"Love and compassion are necessities, not luxuries. Without them humanity cannot survive." ~Dalai Lama

• *The Lemon:* Being insensitive, uncaring, unsympathetic, and callous. Treating people with disrespect leads to a hard, old lemon.

• *Ingredients:* Caring – toward yourself and others. Sensitivity and Empathy – move beyond sympathy, put yourself in someone else's shoes. Respect – Do unto others…. Listening – not just hearing. Loving-kindness – goodwill towards all beings, including yourself.

• *Preparation:* You don't have to be cruel to be kind. Take kindness and caring with a hefty amount of sensitivity and empathy for others. Sympathy alone may lead to general kindness, but the journey to greater compassion requires empathy, heartfelt concern, and loving-kindness built on a background of respect for others. Implicit in this is the art of listening to others. Now remember that the first relationship in which to be compassionate is the one with yourself. Prepare this the same way with self-respect and self-compassion. Listen to yourself and be good to yourself.

• *The Lemonade:* The positive benefits are not limited to those with whom you are already compassionate. As the person being compassionate, you tap into an ocean of positive reimbursements. Becoming sympathetic and empathetic to those you know and those that you don't will help you mentally, physically, and emotionally. It will help improve all of your relationships, including family, friends, and coworkers. Improving relationships at work will in turn enhance your success and satisfaction in your career.

17. Find friends

"A true friend is someone who thinks that you are a good egg even though he knows that you are slightly cracked."
~ Bernard Meltzer

"The friend who can be silent with us in a moment of despair or confusion, who can stay with us in an hour of grief and bereavement, who can tolerate not knowing... not healing, not curing... that is a friend who cares."
~ Henri Nouwen

• *The Lemon:* Being lonely. Feeling lost and perhaps even abandoned. Alone time can be great but not when you really feel a need to spend some quality time with another.

• *Ingredients:* Self-confidence – being self-assured. Energy – lots of oomph. Sociability - a cooperative attitude. Gratitude – truly appreciating that everyone has value. Trust – without this you've got no hope. Altruism – the desire to help others.

• *Preparation:* Healthy social relationships aren't just a nicety, they are critical to happiness. But like happiness, friendship is not a destination but a result of mixing the right ingredients. So which comes first, the happiness or the friends? Both; friends lead to happiness and happier people are more likely to develop healthy friendships. So, let's start with some basic self-confidence that will allow you to go outside of your comfort zone to seek other like-minded folks with whom to hang out. Developing friendships requires a great deal of energy – but it will be worth it. Focus on your sociability, approachability, and altruism. Don't just be willing to help your friends – look forward to it. This will be important to attracting the kind of people that you want to be friends with. Bring gratitude into all of your relationships. Realize that everyone has choices and when they choose to spend time and energy on you, don't take this for granted. Finally, healthy relationships should be built with a strong foundation of trust – by everyone.

- *The Lemonade:* The boost in contentment and improved satisfaction with all aspects of life when you have developed close friendships. There is also the added benefit of an enhanced feeling of security with a warm feeling of safety when you have good friends upon which to rely. Friends will provide you with increased strength – not just emotional and psychological; but also physical. When we engage in activities including sports and hobbies, in the presence of friends our performance is enhanced. If you want to eliminate a bad habit, don't just keep it to yourself; tell a bunch of your friends first. The added positive support will lead to increased resilience and a greater chance of success.

18. Be flexible

"Let no one think that flexibility and a predisposition to compromise is a sign of weakness or a sell-out."
~Paul Kagame

"Prepare yourself for the world, as the athletes used to do for their exercise; oil your mind and your manners, to give them the necessary suppleness and flexibility; strength alone will not do." ~Lord Chesterfield

• *The Lemon:* You are "supposed" to be going to a restaurant, movie or event, but it is sold out, closed or the weather changes. Your night is ruined. You are frustrated, disappointed, and ruminate about this for the rest of the night.

• *Ingredients:* Creativity – look for possibilities and think outside the box. Curiosity – what's next (in a good way). Open-minded - not tolerant but positively open-minded. Good eyes – to see the silver lining. Mindfulness – enjoy the present moment. Self-determination – the belief that you can make changes. Self-confidence – you'll do well under many different conditions. Redefine bad – a non, self-induced change may be a blessing.

• *Preparation:* Creativity leads to flexibility. Curiosity allows you to be encouraged by changes and look forward to them. Be open-minded to the exciting possibilities that await you. Realize that there is no "right" or "wrong" or "how your life is supposed to be". Appreciate the "power of possibility". Try to see the silver lining and blessing in disguise. With good eyes, you'll always be able to find one or make one up. Being mindful allows you to live and enjoy the present moment; which is always good. Being inflexible is being mindless. Dwelling and ruminating on the past. It's gone – get over it! You also should realize that your next action is your choice – even when it seems like it is pre-determined. You can stop and determine it each and every moment. Enjoy that feeling. How powerful is that!

• *The Lemonade:* Going with the flow. Not just being willing to change, but appreciating and even looking forward to change. Many important inventions and discoveries occur because flexible people take advantage of mistakes, errors, and unexpected outcomes. The positive quality of flexibility will lead you down the path of continuous happiness, as you are appreciative of whatever is going on and wherever you happen to be at the time. What a wonderfully fulfilling way to live.

19. Be objective

"Dispassionate objectivity is itself a passion, for the real and for the truth."   ~Abraham Maslow

"Are you really sure that a floor can't also be a ceiling?"
                                                    ~M.C. Escher

• *The Lemon:* Being biased and prejudiced. Looking at life with a single-minded perspective. Subjectivity is typically accompanied by being judgmental – a negatively based habit. This frame of mind closes you off to so many new experiences that it makes me sad just thinking about it.

• *Ingredients:* Open-mind – required to look for possibilities. Modesty – being humble. Humility – a healthy appreciation that you don't know everything. Respect – for others. Empathy – where are they coming from? Fairness – and justice for all.

• *Preparation:* Happy people have high self-esteem; but avoid having an inflated ego or being arrogant. Approach this with an open mind. Add the qualities of modesty and humility. This doesn't mean having poor self-esteem. This simply entails not being arrogant enough to believe that you are always correct. This behavior and mindset is easier if you add a basic respect for others and a likewise assumption that they may be correct. In addition to respect, you will be more objective if you bring empathy to the table. Once you have the ability to look at life through someone else's eyes, you will be much better at approaching situations in a fair and nonjudgmental manner.

•   *The Lemonade:* Being non-judgmental. The results are having an open mind and being excited about looking at other possibilities and potentials. Becoming more objective will lead to greater flexibility and being more approachable to others. Elevated objectivity will also induce other positive changes such as making new friends and feeling better about situations in which you find yourself. In addition, you will be more comfortable with decisions made by others.

20. Try new things

"Don't fear failure so much that you refuse to try new things. The saddest summary of a life contains three descriptions: could have, might have, and should have."

~Louis E. Boone

"Do not go where the path may lead; go instead where there is no path and leave a trail."

~ Ralph Waldo Emerson

• *The Lemon:* Being satisfied with having things and doing things the way that they have always been done. Lack of innovation. Lack of new experiences. Not finding or appreciating novel ideas or experiences. Being ruled by fear and living in the past. Old lemonade.

• *Ingredients:* <u>Innovation</u> – finding beauty in novelty. <u>Passion</u> – for new experience. <u>Courage</u> – to go beyond your comfort zone. <u>Creativity</u> – an active imagination. <u>Hope</u> – for great experiences. <u>Belief</u> - that they will come true.

• *Preparation:* Truth be told, a little creativity helps but more importantly, look at everything and everyday and every minute as new. This moment is not the same as the last. In reality, doing the same activity today as I did yesterday is not the exact same thing if I approach it with a new and fresh outlook. But, have the courage to go beyond the tried and true. When you go to the same favorite restaurant, try something that you've never had before, something that would surprise your friends and family.

Be creative. Try it with hope and the belief that it will be something wonderful. Go on a ride that you would not normally do. Go to a store or market that you wouldn't typically visit. Go to the opera. Go to the ballet. TRY SOMETHING NEW!

• *The Lemonade:* Brand-new lemonade. Everything old is new again – if you look at every day and all things with a fresh new outlook. Everything is approached in a new, innovative or novel way. One of the proven methods to increase long-term happiness is to use your top strengths in **new** ways. Don't focus on your fears but on your potential. When you do this, how would it be possible for everything to not seem great? The answer is that it wouldn't be possible – everything would be wonderful.

21. Love yourself

"I don't like myself, I'm crazy about myself." ~ Mae West

"If you aren't good at loving yourself, you will have a difficult time loving anyone, since you'll resent the time and energy you give another person that you aren't even giving to yourself." ~ Barbara De Angelis

• *The Lemon:* Not being comfortable in your own shoes. Wishing you were *somewhere* or *someone* else. You wish you were someone else, but guess what? Everyone else is already taken. When you don't truly care for who you are – that's a lemon.

• *Ingredients:* Self-appreciation – approval for who you are. Self-esteem – admire yourself. Patience – with your faults. Forgiveness – for your mistakes. Pride – in who you are. Emotional and Social Intelligence – How well do you know yourself?

• *Preparation:* Liking yourself is good. Loving yourself is better. You can make a mistake and be mad at yourself. But don't let that change your opinion of who you are. Give yourself the gift of patience and forgiveness. If you aren't happy with whom you are, make a change. You have that power. No one else can make you change. Make positive changes with a goal of loving yourself openly and honestly. Do things that you are proud of and be proud of what you do. If it would make your mother proud of you, it's probably a good thing.

• *The Lemonade:* Looking at yourself with open eyes and really appreciating who you are. Knowing yourself and loving what you see in the mirror. This doesn't mean that you must think that you are perfect looking or that you are the prettiest or most handsome. But it means that you are fully and happily accepting of the kind of person that you see in the mirror looking back at you. When you love yourself, this will be obvious to others and you will start attracting like-minded positive people into your circle of friends.

22. Love others

"Being deeply loved by someone gives you strength, while loving someone deeply gives you courage."

~ Lao Tzu

•   *The Lemon:* Not feeling close to those around you; being critical of others. Erecting barriers to prevent your relationships from actually becoming truly meaningful and loving.

•   *Ingredients:* Humility – being truly humble. Kindness – of the loving kind. Respect. Empathy. Genuineness – an authentic you. Altruism – a spirit of generosity. Emotional and Social Intelligence – how well do you know others? Interest – focused awareness. Inspiration – motivation to transcend the ordinary. Awe – overwhelmed by greatness. Grateful – for the gift of others. Enjoyment – be amused. Behavioral Synchrony – how well we "click" with others.

•   *Preparation:* Before you can begin to think about this recipe, you need to have successfully made the preceding recipe – Love Yourself. There are essential techniques and ingredients found in loving yourself that you will need in loving others. The act of love utilizes many interpersonal strengths such as empathy, altruism, trust, kindness, and respect. Indeed, it is a many splendored thing. Understanding others' viewpoints and a nonjudgmental willingness and ability to see things through the eyes of another. Loving others entails the ability and want to help, forgive, trust, and respect other people in an open and honest fashion. If you can't do this with authenticity, it just won't be magic! Loving others entails finding joy and amusement in a relationship and being grateful for, inspired by and interested in the gifts and talents of others. The psychologist, Barbara Fredrickson has described love as "positive resonance", involving behavioral synchrony – "clicking" with others. This comes about through connectedness – eye contact, voice, and touch.

• *The Lemonade:* The ultimate experience. The feeling of "you get me". One of the 10 components of Dr. Fredrickson's Positivity. She has also described love as an interpersonally situated and socially shared experience involving one or more positive emotions. We invest in the well-being of others and create life-enhancing, mutual bonds. It engulfs so much of who we are as social animals. It converts casual acquaintances to beautiful, heartfelt relationships. This profoundly, passionate affection for another person will help fulfill some of your emotional, mental, and physical needs. Most importantly, you will be providing spiritual nutrition for your soul.

23. Practice humility

"If I only had a little humility, I would be perfect."
~Ted Turner

• *The Lemon:* Being proud, arrogant, conceited, and pompous. Putting yourself above others with a false sense of pride.

• *Ingredients:* <u>Admiration</u>. <u>Respect</u>. <u>Appreciation</u> – for others. <u>Modesty</u> – unpretentious humility. <u>Moderation</u> – just say no to excess.

• *Preparation:* Do something out of the goodness of your heart. Not because it is self-serving. Humility is basically a freedom from you thinking about you. This is not self-deprecating behavior for the purpose of receiving praise. I am not saying that you should not recognize your talents, strengths, abilities and virtues. But it is also important to recognize the talents, strengths, abilities, and virtues that others possess. Acknowledging the aptitude and capabilities of others is a great step on the first rung of the humility ladder. Now add two mod self-mastery strengths: *mod*eration - resisting temptations and refraining from pretentious and arrogant behavior and *mod*esty – knowing and appreciating that you are not perfect and that others can and do possess some remarkable abilities.

• *The Lemonade:* There are over 6.8 billion people in the world. That means that even if you're a "one-in-million" type of person, there are still over six thousand, eight hundred people like you. Have a disposition to be humble. Humility is considered a virtue in many religious and philosophical traditions. This doesn't mean not being honest about yourself. It does not mean putting yourself down or claiming that you are lower than others. It simply refers to not having or exhibiting a false sense of pride. In Buddhism, humility liberates you from the sufferings of life and the displeasures of the mind. Enlightenment comes only after humility. Come and get enlightened!

24. *Exercise self-control*

"The happiness of a man in this life does not consist in the absence but in the mastery of his passions."

~ Alfred, Lord Tennyson

• *The Lemon:* Your self-indulgence makes you feel satisfied in the short term but unfulfilled and discontented in the long term. You give into cravings, addictions, temptation, impulsivity, or deprivation that results in imbalance and harm to your body and soul.

• *Ingredients:* <u>Emotional intelligence</u> – who are you really? <u>Moderation</u> – when is enough, enough? <u>Modesty</u> – a little humility never hurt anyone. <u>Self-discipline</u> – restraint. <u>Balance</u> – in all aspects of life.

• *Preparation:* You can't have it all – well, maybe you can, but you shouldn't. It's not good for you; besides where would you put it? Goal-setting is important but lack of balance and perspective during goal-setting is unhealthy. Learn more about yourself. Try to understand what makes you tick and what motivates you to do the things that you do. Appreciate that you have cravings and desires that may not be good to fulfill. Use your strengths in moderation, modesty, and self-restraint to control those temptations and addictions. As soon as you are able to conquer unreasonable impulses, you will feel yourself starting to find balance in life. Your self-confidence, self-acceptance, and love for self will skyrocket. Try it – you'll like it!

- *The Lemonade:* Avoiding extremes is the first step on the road to finding balance; emotional, physical, mental, spiritual, and psychological balance. Doing positive things (such as working toward a goal – being promoted at work), is a great thing. But pursuing that goal at the exclusion of important relationships and in place of your physical health and spiritual nutrition is going to be more harmful than beneficial. Exercising self-discipline and self-control will leave you well-balanced with a good sense of perspective. You will be more open-minded, flexible, and enhance your approachability – the road to developing new friends. Simply achieving the realization that you are in control of your destiny is hugely empowering.

25. *Realize that only you can choose*

"It is impossible for you to be angry and laugh at the same time. Anger and laughter are mutually exclusive and you have the power to choose either."
~Wayne Dyer

"The one thing you can't take away from me is the way I choose to respond to what you do to me. The last of one's freedoms is to choose ones attitude in any given circumstance." ~Viktor Frankl

• *The Lemon:* Giving up control. Either not realizing or pretending that you are not in charge of your own life. You will blame others and complain about things that you can do something about. This will negatively affect all of your relationships, your drive to succeed, and your satisfaction with your career, your life, and yourself.

• *Ingredients:* Self-acceptance – you are the only you. Self-confidence – in your ability to make decisions and take action. Forgiveness - yourself. Flexibility – in your thoughts and plans. Responsibility and Accountability – for your thoughts, feelings and actions.

• *Preparation:* Accept who you are in a realistic fashion. Be confident in who you are and have confidence that you will make the right decisions. Be kind to yourself and forgive yourself when you don't make the right decisions or be flexible in your journey and willing to adapt to where that decision leads you. Be responsible and accountable; you are your own master of ceremonies. Show gratitude more than blame.

- *The Lemonade:* Being self-actualized in the realization that you do have ultimate control of your reality. You can choose so many more things for which you have ever given yourself credit. As stated in the introduction in this book, if you aren't happy with someone or something, you can always change *it.* Sometimes the *it* refers to the something or someone. Sometimes the *it* refers to the not being happy. The old expression, "Do you want to change your mind...or are you happy with the mind you have?" You and you alone have the ability and the strength to change your perspective and perceptions. This knowledge is not only enlightening but also empowering. You'll be taking large gulps of this lemonade.

Neil E. Farber, M.D., PhD.

26. Realize your awesome potential

"Everyone has inside of him a piece of good news. The good news is that you don't know how great you can be! How much you can love! What you can accomplish! And what your potential is!" ～Anne Frank

• *The Lemon:* Not appreciating how much potential you have. Not being able to achieve optimal experiences. When you don't understand how far you can travel along a road, you are more likely to take an early turn on the road and not reach your goal.

• *Ingredients:* Intrinsic motivation – the drive comes from within. Goal-directed behavior – acting with purpose. Patience – it won't happen all at once. Determination – to complete the task. Self-confidence – sure you can. Resilience – ain't no turning back, roll with the punches. Hope – keeps us moving forward.

• *Preparation:* Reach out of your comfort zone. Bring with you the resilience to not be thwarted by apparent obstacles; you can overcome them. When you possess the faith, hope, determination, and knowledge that you can achieve amazing things; and that it is your destiny to do so, obstacles and problems will transition into do-able challenges. Have the patience to see it through – it will be worth it. This process may take some time, but then again, most things that are worthwhile are time consuming.

- *The Lemonade:* People with an orientation to achieving self-actualization ("being" orientation), rather than a goal of obtaining stuff ("having" orientation), are happier. Choosing to pursue goals that are personally meaningful and intrinsically-motivated such as self-actualizing, results in greater subjective well-being and that exhilarating feeling of awe for which we all search. So focus on "being" rather than "doing". Remember, you are not just a human doing, you are also a human being.

27. Practice positive thinking

"The positive thinker sees the invisible, feels the intangible, and achieves the impossible."

~Author unknown

- *The Lemon:* The glass of lemonade is half empty. When you think negative thoughts, you will often get what you wish for. Our lives are, in large part, determined by our thoughts. Our thoughts influence our words, which influence our actions and behaviors. Negative thoughts will distract your focus, drain your energy, and reduce your chance of success; in relationships, careers, family and life.

- *Ingredients:* Belief – that things are good now. Hope – faith that things will get even better. Optimism – your self-talk, Deep Breath – be active, not reactive. Meditate – focused thought and perhaps some relaxation. Curiosity and Creativity – look for the good. Respect – for others and yourself. Mindfulness – continuous attention to what you are thinking. Perseverance and Resilience – keep on truckin'.

- *Preparation:* Read positive quotes. Hang out with positive people. Believe in and try to appreciate how good things truly are. Realize that you have the ability to control your thoughts – make use of that ability. Maintain hope for a beautiful future. Practice optimism. When things go wrong, positive people regard it as being temporary, limited and beyond their control; while good things are thought of as being permanent and pervasive. When frustrated or upset, take a deep breath and relax before you respond. Try to meditate or use other techniques that help you relax. Use your curiosity and creativity to search for and seek out the good in all situations and interactions. Know that you can find positivity in apparently negative situations. You need to include a respect for yourself. If you want the best for yourself, you need to stay in the positive zone. You also need a respect for others. This will help you be more positive about your feelings toward friends, family, coworkers and especially strangers. Don't be lazy. Focusing on positive thoughts requires you to be mindful of all your thoughts and feelings. It takes sustained effort and fortitude; so don't give up. For long-lasting results, turn positive thinking into a habit – not a time-limited activity for a few minutes per day.

• *The Lemonade:* The glass of lemonade is half full. Positive thinking plays an important role in affecting positive outcome. Similar to a placebo effect, positive thoughts alone may increase endogenous pain-relieving chemicals. What starts off as "all in your mind" quickly moves to being in your body as well – and it feels really great. If something is not in line with your hopes and dreams for the future; throw it out! Happiness increases by consciously adapting certain thought patterns and habits. Adopting these positive thoughts will be like getting a high power energy boost. Warning: this is addictive lemonade.

Neil E. Farber, M.D., PhD.

28. *Practice positive emotions*

"You will not be punished for your anger. You'll be punished by your anger." ~ Buddhist quote

- *The Lemon:* Negative emotional health can ruin your whole day. As an integral part of the mind-body connection, you'll have a weaker immune system; more frequent infections. You'll likely experience more back pain, ulcers, headaches, high blood pressure, insomnia, sexual problems, bowel problems, and palpitations. You'll have difficulties exercising, eating, and developing or maintaining close relationships. A very unhealthy lemon.

- *Ingredients:* Self-awareness, Self – control and Emotional Intelligence – who are you really. Compassionate and Empathetic – walk in someone else's shoes. Resilience – don't be thwarted. Flexibility – change is good. Amusement and Joy – try to find it everywhere. Calm – amidst turmoil.

- *Preparation:* The mind-body connection is real and it is powerful. Be aware of your own emotional status. Even "good" change can be stressful. You'll reduce the stress and anxiety of change if you have the flexibility to adapt to new situations and seek out the joy, amusement, or humor that is potentially hidden in all these situations. It takes a special person to find these hidden treasures. You are that special person. Reacting emotionally often leads to overreacting emotionally resulting in conflicts and poor relationships. Try to understand your emotional status and how it relates to those around you. Be compassionate and empathetic to others and you will both be the beneficiaries of your positive emotional state. Above all else be calm and calming. This will help put things in perspective and balance.

• *The Lemonade:* People practicing positive emotions have learned healthy ways to cope with stress and anxieties that will deter others. They have strong and lasting relationships. They feel good about and accept who they are. Changes occur continuously for all of us. Those with positive emotional health are more easily able to adapt to those changes and find the amusement and hope in whatever outcome that change may forecast. Putting positive emotions together with positive thoughts is much more likely to result in positive speech (see next chapter).

29. Practice positive speech

"People who say it cannot be done should not interrupt those who are doing it." ~Anonymous

- *The Lemon:* In Hebrew this is known as Lashon Hara. Evil tongue. Speaking badly of someone or something. The use of negative speech is more detrimental to the speaker than to the subject of the negativity.

- *Ingredients:* <u>Mindfulness</u> – be aware of your words. <u>Respect</u> - for others. <u>Humility</u> –be humble. <u>Self-respect and self-acceptance</u> – like yourself before trying to like the rest of the world. <u>Edit</u> – before you speak. <u>Responsibility</u> - no excuses. <u>Proper speech</u> – ethical speech, do no harm. <u>Gratitude</u> – say, "thanks". <u>Forgiveness</u> – move beyond blame. <u>Accountability</u> - say, "sorry".

- *Preparation:* How we speak about others has profound relationship effects. Undergo a speech makeover. Be mindful of what you are saying. Start with your thoughts that influence your words. Choose words from a positive perspective. Believe in the goodness of people while you are speaking of them. Remember, nobody *makes* you say anything. What comes out of your mouth is completely up to you. To say or think otherwise is to give up control of your words, your destiny and your life. You need to be satisfied with who you are before you can elevate to speaking well of others. Don't rationalize negative speech. You can edit your words before they hit the airwaves. Use ethical speech.

Don't speak badly of others or gossip. Don't say anything about anyone that you wouldn't honestly say directly to them and that you wouldn't want someone to say about you. Two powerfully positive forms of speech are those involved in showing gratitude and forgiveness – practice them often.

The Lemonade: Positive words and phrases reprogram your mind and initiate positive behaviors. They inhibit negative ruminations and give others their first glimpse of your positive and attractive nature. You will become a glowing source of affirmation and power that people will want to tap into rather than an energy drain that people want to run away from. The physical, emotional, and spiritual health benefits from simply practicing the arts of gratitude and forgiveness are amazing. When you start practicing positive speak, it won't take long before you see all of your relationships begin to flourish. This will be a positive feedback loop as you are duly rewarded for your healthful words.

30. Practice positive actions

"Vision without action is a dream. Action without vision is simply passing the time. Action with Vision is making a positive difference."
~Joel Barker

• *The Lemon:* Inactivity and idleness. Laziness and boredom. Bad Habits. Bad Lemons.

• *Ingredients:* Positive action words – use them for organizing your thoughts. Self-confidence – you know that you can. Determination – don't stop until you achieve your goal. Motivation – to make things better. Fortitude – resilience. Hope and Faith – that you can make a difference. Create – new ways of doing old things. Curious – how can you take ownership of this activity? Altruism – helping others. Oxytocin – for a helper's high.

• *Preparation:* As you prepare to take action, focus on positive action words such as succeed, complete, create, and achieve. Incorporate these words into your activities. Add a hefty amount of self-confidence and determination. Set your goal before you begin. Don't get frustrated when confronted with challenges, rise to the occasion and be determined to complete the task. You'll need motivation and fortitude to see this through and these will come, in part, through your endless hope and faith in the greater good of what you are trying to achieve. Be creative and curious – don't be limited to the tried and true. When you are passionate about effecting positive change, you will find new and improved ways of making them happen. While not all positive actions involve others, being altruistic is certainly a great way to kick-off a positivity activity. Accompanying the act of helping others is a release of the "tend and befriend" hormone, oxytocin – add a few heaping tablespoons.

• *The Lemonade:* Positive thoughts to positive words to positive actions. Participating in positive behaviors, leads to positive self-assessments and feelings, which in turn, causes positive thoughts – the positive cycle of life! Positive actions allow us to pursue goals, make healthy decisions, and practice good habits. Through the use of positive actions we are able to exhibit resilience, conquer fears and go where we've never gone before. Positive actions help and show gratitude to other people. Practicing positive actions will always make your life more satisfying and meaningful.

Making Lemonade

APPETIZERS

31. Don't just love yourself, like yourself?

"Have the courage to say no. Have the courage to face the truth. Do the right thing because it is right. These are the magic keys to living your life with integrity."
~ W. Clement Stone

• *The Lemon:* Feeling sorry for yourself. Not being able to look in the mirror for fear of what might be staring back at you. Low self-esteem. Being highly critical of yourself and actively self-flagellating. An ugly lemon.

• *Ingredients:* Integrity - honor, truth and trustworthy. Conviction – believe in you. Courage – to face the truth. Acceptance – of self. Forgiveness – you'll never be perfect and you don't have to be. Self-awareness and Mindfulness – regarding your thoughts and feelings.

• *Preparation:* Give yourself approval to follow your heart and the freedom and acceptance to be who you are. Have the courage and conviction to know that when you are on the right path, don't be derailed. Live as if your mother sees *everything* that you do (because she probably does). Don't worry about your reputation – that's what other people think of you. Instead, worry about your character – that's who you really are. You aren't perfect. I'm not perfect. Admit it and be comfortable with that. Be prepared to forgive yourself; you can't be happy and continually self-criticize. You'll make mistakes; let it go. Learn from them and move on. Don't lie to yourself. Have integrity and admit when you are trying to pull the wool over your eyes. Have the courage to face the truth and the courage to change if you don't like what you see. To like yourself, you have to know yourself. Mindfully be aware of your thoughts and emotions. Remember you can also control them.

• *The Lemonade:* Seeing a bright, shining smile reflected in the mirror. Be a first-class version of yourself; not a second-class version of somebody else. Remember, everybody else is already taken. There is maybe no better feeling in the world than the feeling that you are not unduly proud, but that you are wholly comfortable with yourself and that you actually like who, what and where (spiritually, emotionally, and metaphysically) you are.

32. *Get off the hedonic elliptical machine*

"Like the proverbial rats, we run faster and faster — and so do our aspirations — but the bottom line is the old cliché: Money can't buy happiness." ~Andrew L. Yarrow

• *The Lemon:* You try and you try to get things that will make you happy. You even won the lottery. Yes, you're richer, but alas, you're no happier now than you were before. Just like the elliptical machine, you work and you work to make things better, but in the end, you're in the same place as when you started. No matter how good it seems to be, we adapt. Your economic expectations and desires rise at the same rate as your income – but there is no net gain of satisfaction or happiness. As Positive Psychologist, Ed Diener has shown, happiness has not risen in western nations in the last 50 years despite massive increases in monetary gain.

• *Ingredients:* <u>Meditation</u> – it keeps getting better with time. <u>Comparisons</u> – with some and not with others. <u>Happiness</u> - not pleasure. <u>Creativity</u> – what else can you do with money. <u>Altruism</u> – generosity. <u>Autonomy</u> – you are the agent of change. <u>Virtuous</u> – a life worth living.

• *Preparation:* Participating in activities which continually change, such as meditation – where each session will be different in some way, regenerates positivity and converts the hedonic elliptical machine to an escalator that actually transports you upward. In general, tried to avoid comparisons. However, they may be important to make when they are with those less fortunate than ourselves. This will remind you to be thankful for what you have and perhaps even to spend less on unnecessary material things. Comparing ourselves to others and trying to keep up with the Joneses and with the current standard of what we "should" have, contributes to the hedonic elliptical. Focus your efforts on doing things that make you happy, not simply create pleasure – which is fleeting and externally driven. Money isn't all evil. Be creative in the use of money. Spend it on a nice vacation, going out with family and friends, photo albums, etc.

• *The Lemonade:* The Kingdom of Bhutan has jumped off the hedonic elliptical machine and instead of gross domestic product, they now measure the country's success based on gross national happiness. Spending money on philanthropy and altruistic activities will help you jump off the elliptical and onto the escalator. You have the ability to make the changes and when you focus on living a virtuous life, happiness is more likely to follow.

33. Keep a gratitude journal

"When you are grateful fear disappears and abundance appears."
~Anthony Robbins

• *The Lemon:* When you're upset, someone else is to blame. When you're happy, how come you alone are responsible? Ingratitude. Ungrateful. Thankless. Alone…

• *Ingredients:* Awareness – of who has helped. Journal – doesn't have to be anything fancy. Recognition and Acknowledgement - don't take anything or anyone for granted. Appreciation – for your blessings. Humility – others' help. Memories – don't limit yourself to now. Time – not a whole lot. Routine – it's not a one-time thing. Sharing – with a loved one.

• *Preparation:* Continuously be aware of what you are thankful for and to whom you would like to thank. Everyday keep track in a notebook or journal, people, companies, corporations, and organizations to whom you are grateful. Count your blessings and try to attribute the cause of this good fortune to someone or something. Attribute your good fortune and positive characteristics to those who have helped you in the past get to where you are now (even from a bad place); or perhaps something specific that occurred today. These can be in the form of brief blessings or notes; directed to individuals, groups, spiritual figures, God, the universe or Mother Nature. Make this a nightly habit. It will improve your sleep when the last thing on your mind is positive appraisal.

Examples: I am so grateful that...*I am in good health.*

...I have great friends...I have good vision...I have the ability to see, hear, smell and touch...My family is healthy.

I am thankful for the opportunity to...*go fishing...go to work...eat this great meal...see my children grow up.*

I am so thankful that my loved ones...*live so close...are healthy...have good families...have wonderful values.*

• *The Lemonade:* Nothing is too small. The more things for which you are thankful, the greater your appreciation for others and for your life. This has become a very popular assignment in positive psychology courses and a well-accepted and simple technique to raise happiness levels. When you read over your gratitude journal, you'll be able to focus on all of the positive aspects of your life and the positive support that you have that has helped you achieve these items and characteristics. To create sweeter lemonade; share your gratitude journal with your spouse or significant other. The effects are profound and relationship strengthening. Keeping a gratitude journal for just three weeks will help your sleep and give you an energy boost.

34. Write gratitude letters

"Feeling gratitude and not expressing it is like wrapping a present and not giving it." ~ William Arthur Ward

• *The Lemon:* Either feeling ungrateful or feeling grateful and keeping it to yourself. Gratitude unexpressed is a no thank you.

• *Ingredients:* <u>Awareness</u> – who is deserving? <u>Memory</u> – who is deserving? <u>People</u> – who are deserving? <u>Appreciation</u> – count your blessings. <u>Humility</u> – important step to gratefulness. <u>Sincerity</u> – your genuineness will shine through. <u>Paper and Pen</u> or a <u>Computer and Email</u>.

• *Preparation:* This is a letter to a specific person or group of people who has (have) positively impacted your life. A person from the present or the past. (1) Try to write a letter within a few days of an event. (2) State specifically what the person did to teach you, help you, inspire you, direct you, etc. (3) Tell them what qualities you appreciate about them such as leadership, humor, honesty, generosity, etc. (4) Express your feelings of thankfulness toward them. How what they did made a difference in your life. People respond positively when treated kindly. Employees work harder when they feel appreciated.

Some sample phrases: congratulations on..., have taught me so much about..., did such a great job..., am very proud of the way..., for your steadfast support of..., have great admiration for..., have wonderful insight..., have renewed my faith in..., how thankful I have been for..., how much I admire... your ability to..., not sure how you managed to..., the way you..., have a gift for..., for your kindness..., for being there..., are a great friend..., making a great contribution..., gave me the incentive to..., your extraordinary sensitivity about..., especially appreciate..., if it hadn't been for you...the amazing job that you did..., was thrilled to discover...

Now that you've finished your letter, reap the most positive benefit possible; hand-deliver it. That is, make a gratitude visit. Imagine how great it would feel to have a letter of appreciation written to you and then how much better it would feel having it brought to you. What a great relationship builder.

• *The Lemonade:* "As we express our gratitude, we must never forget that the highest appreciation is not to utter words, but to live by them." ~ John Fitzgerald Kennedy. People who practice grateful thinking can increase their happiness set-point by 25 percent. We're talking big-time changes. Like gratitude journaling, writing gratitude letters can improve your heart, soul, and happiness. Gratitude is more than just a pleasant feeling. It causes long-term happiness and heartfelt appreciation.

35. Become aware of your breathing

"If you know the techniques of mindful breathing, mindful walking, mindful smiling, you can bring your mind back to your body and you become truly alive."
~ Thich Nhat Hanh

• *The Lemon:* Mindlessness – the world goes around and you don't know it. You breathe over 20,000 times per day and are hardly aware of all but a few of these. Going through the day without appreciating who you are or what you are thinking, feeling, doing, or sensing.

• *Ingredients:* Chair or Floor space. Awareness - of your senses.

• *Preparation:* Sit in a relatively comfortable position. Without changing your breathing pattern, gently bring your attention to your breathing and make a mental note of how you inspire and expire. Observe the natural rhythm of your breathing. When your mind wanders, allow it to do so and gently redirect it back to your breathing. Every breath in is spiritually and physically nourishing to your body and soul. The breath carries essential oxygen to nourishing cells. Breathing is at the junction of voluntary and automatic activities. When we concentrate on our breathing, we are focusing on the present moment. There are several wonderful mindful breathing techniques to try; each with a different focus and benefit, such as 1) recognizing breathing – just being aware of your natural breathing, 2) awareness of the length of the breath (without adjusting it), 3) alternate nostril breathing – use a finger to close one nostril at a time (4) abdominal (diaphragmatic) breathing – place hand below your navel and feel it rise as you inhale deeply, 5) counting breaths – usually sets of 10, 6) following a breath – visualizing the air moving in your nose and throughout the respiratory pathway until it exists again through the nose, 7) mindful breathing while walking, 8) mindful breathing while "impartially watching" other senses, or your thoughts or your physical body – stay detached and open.

•   *The Lemonade:* Being aware of your thoughts, feelings, actions, and sensations. Becoming aware of your breathing is the first step on the road to being deeply centered and having a quiet, contented mind. This mindfulness practice will help you learn to focus and concentrate on many other facets of your life. Coming back to the breathing is the foundation of mindfulness practice. Breath awareness activates the mind-body connection; creating a sense of wholeness, clarity, insight, and harmony.

36. *Don't go to bed mad - often*

"For every minute you are angry, you lose sixty seconds of happiness." ⁓Author Unknown

• *The Lemon:* Anger hurts the sender just as much as the recipient. Nothing gets solved while expressing anger. Anger is one letter away from Danger. The adrenaline rush that you experience while you are angry, creates more anger and in a relationship this soon leads to danger.

• *Ingredients:* Deep breathe – calming. Respect – for others. Empathy – combine sympathy and understanding. Emotional intelligence – being perceptive of others' emotions. Self-control – you don't need to express everything. Humility – you may be wrong! Self-Preservation – hurting others hurts you.

• *Preparation:* It's a myth that not working through every conflict immediately will cause it to grow and take on a life of its own. There are rare times where you may need to sleep on it and cool off before approaching a heated subject. However, getting yourself into a calmer place (internally calmer) right away will always help you work out differences and disagreements. Letting off steam is not the solution – it's part of the problem. So, it's better to go to bed mad than to say or do something that you'll regret later. But the best solution is to not retain the anger. Problem solve with your partner. Try to assume that there is something about the story that you don't know or understand. Focus on "the ultimate goal". If your goal is to win the argument, realize that you may get your wish. Win the argument, but lose the relationship in the process – makes for many long, cold nights. If your goal is to attain and maintain a loving, close relationship, then step up to the plate, calm down, and try to understand and empathize. Precede with the mindset that this is someone who cares for you and whom you respect. When you use words that hurt them, you are really hurting your relationship which, in turn hurts you. It can take five positive comments to undo the anger-causing effect of one negative remark.

• *The Lemonade:* Realizing that what seemed to be a big problem was a little misunderstanding. Lying in bed calm, relaxed with pleasant thoughts and motivated to see what excitement tomorrow will bring. This is not a fake happiness that comes from ignoring anger and feelings of resentment. This is true contentment that comes from peacefully resolving conflicts. A wonderful feeling followed by a restful sleep.

37. Don't compare

"In order to be utterly happy the only thing necessary is to refrain from comparing this moment with other moments in the past, which I often did not fully enjoy because I was comparing them with other moments of the future". ~Andre Gide

• *The Lemon:* Spend your time thinking about how great it was in the past and how great it will be in the future. You're missing the best time ever – right now! Daydreaming is a temporary distraction from the amazing things going on around you.

• *Ingredients:* <u>Mindfulness</u> – awareness of the present. <u>Openness</u> and <u>Interest</u> – to the experience. <u>Receptivity</u> – non-judgmentally. <u>Flexibility</u> and <u>Adaptability</u> – change happens all the time. <u>Commitment</u> – to now.

• *Preparation:* Start with an awareness of your breathing and your senses. Move to an awareness of your body, your thoughts, and your mind. Become aware of where you are and what you are doing; nonjudgmentally. Be open, interested, and receptive to all that you perceive. Be flexible and adaptable to changing or unexpected situations. Do all of these things with a commitment to the people, places, and things in which you are involved. You go to a restaurant and remark how great the steak is. Then you remember that the best steaks in the world are at a little place in Rome, Italy. Guess what? Your steak doesn't taste as good as it did a second ago. Now instead, after remarking how great the steak is, you remember how bad the steak was last week at another restaurant. You might think that this will enhance the steak experience now but it won't because your mind has brought you into the past and you're no longer here enjoying this steak!

• *The Lemonade:* You can't compare anything without living in the past or the future. When you stop comparing you can focus on the here and now. Put your full attention and commitment to the present time, situations, events, activities and people. You will always feel more fulfilled when you are focused on the now. Studying new things like languages becomes easier and more fun. You will learn better in school and perform better at your job. It's also a great technique to improve safety. Imagine how much better it is to drive, fly planes, and operate heavy machinery when you are not thinking of how much nicer tomorrow will be when you're on vacation. Wouldn't you prefer that your pilot is completely mindful about flying rather than comparing? Previously mundane activities will seem more exciting and satisfying. Intrinsically stimulating activities will be downright exhilarating! It will be readily apparent to anyone that you interact with, that you are truly focused on them. This will positively enhance all of your relationships.

38. Be patient

"If I have ever made any valuable discoveries, it has been owning more to patient attention, than to any other talent."
~Isaac Newton

• *The Lemon:* Losing your temper, becoming easily irritated, annoyed and short-tempered.

• *Ingredients:* Endurance - wait it out. Fortitude – don't give up. Hope and Faith – without these strengths you'll not be able to create patience. Self-compassion – be kind to yourself. Goals – they take time to accomplish. Compassion and Tolerance – toward others. Self-control – restraint and discipline.

• *Preparation:* We live in a "I want it now" society. But, good things take time to develop; time to flourish; time to mature; time to reveal themselves. You must not lose hope and faith that these changes and rewards will occur. Have fortitude to continue with what you know is right. Have confidence in the system, in others and in yourself that you will accomplish your goals. Being tolerant and open-minded is an important step in the development of patience. Patience is impossible without the restraint and discipline that accompanies self-control. When you start to feel anxious about achieving a goal, remember that impatience leads to more fear and anxiety. Don't go there.

• *The Lemonade:* Patience is an art to be practiced. When you practice patience, you develop confidence and decisiveness. You can step back and rationally evaluate a situation, improving your chances of success. Patience converts quick, mindless reactions to contemplated, calculated, mindful actions. Don't forget to have patience with yourself when you need some time to create, develop, or just be and not do for a while. Patience allows you to see the big picture. Sometimes it really pays to wait for the fruit to ripen before picking it. While you're using your patience, take advantage of the opportunity to research, learn, focus, relax, grow, and goal-set.

39. Give compliments

"I can live for two months on a good compliment."
~Mark Twain

- *The Lemon:* Not feeling thankful. Not feeling or exhibiting appreciation to others. Being too proud, self-absorbed or having expectations that are too high to praise others.

- *Ingredients:* <u>Focus</u> - on someone else. <u>Investigation</u> – explore the possibilities for praise. <u>Creative</u> – come up with something new. <u>Inquiry</u> – find out who was responsible for something that you liked. <u>Genuineness</u> – being honest and open. <u>Altruism</u> – giving from your heart. <u>Kindness</u> and <u>Compassion</u> – can't create a compliment lemonade without these. <u>Gracious words</u> – given away for free.

- *Preparation:* Actively search for positive traits in everyone that you meet. Look for attributes and specific examples of good deeds or helpful activities. This isn't for special occasions. Make this a habit and a regular occurrence. Giving compliments at least three to five times per day, you'll begin to appreciate how people are truly multifaceted. You'll find that you are looking for the best in people. Do this with kindness and compassion. Be honest and receptive to people. It takes little time and no money. The amount of exertion may seem moderate at first, but after a little practice, the effort is truly minimal. What gracious words to use? Think of positive values, positive character traits and positive strengths. Now find them in others. Words like *Smart,*

Brave, Honest, Kind, Helpful, Fair, Forgiving, Reliable, Self-confident, Motivating, Friendly, Creative, Hard worker, Generous, Caring, Good sport, Common sense, Giving, Loyal, Genuine, Compassionate, Self-disciplined, etc. In many jobs the only critiques from bosses to employees is when things go wrong. Change that! Send a compliment (when it is justified). What a way to improve attitudes and relationships and become more engaged in work.

• *The Lemonade:* Connecting honestly, kindly and directly with another person. Compliments are an essential ingredient in solidifying relationships. It will positively change the way you view the world, other people, and your connectedness with them. The paradox is that as you compliment others, you will build your own self-confidence and self-acceptance. Giving and helping others helps the giver at least as much as the getter. Giving compliments is no exception. You will feel happier and more satisfied. Looking for the best in people will spill over to other aspects of your life. You'll be looking for the positive and possibilities in everything that happens.

40. *Learn something new every day*

"I don't think much of a man who is not wiser today than he was yesterday." ~Abraham Lincoln

• *The Lemon:* Cockiness or laziness or self-satisfied. Mindless. Stale lemons. When you stop learning – you're done. Pack it up and sit in your room…alone…in the dark…with an Edgar Allen Poe poem. Assume that you either know everything or not interested in learning more? Dangerous lemons!

• *Ingredients:* Awareness and Mindfulness – everything old is new again. Open and Receptive – to new things, people and events. Questions and Curiosity – rather than answers and knowledge.

• *Preparation:* Don't worship what you know; question it. The first step to learning something new is simply to pay attention and becoming aware. It is impossible to be mindful and not learn something new. In fact, if you are truly mindful, you are probably learning something new every second. It's pretty darn exciting! Walk around like you have something new to learn. You will be seen as open, receptive and approachable. It's harder to learn something from people who agree with you. Don't take the easy road; it will be worthwhile. Be challenged. Take new paths. Go places and do things that you've only thought about experiencing. If you're too old to learn, you were probably always too old to learn. Learning has nothing to do with age and everything to do with attitude and fortitude. Asking questions with the goal of learning and the attitude of gaining knowledge. Realize of course that everything that we learn could be incorrect and we must look just as passionately at the process of relearning. If what you learn today was that what you learned yesterday was not correct, then it was indeed a great day. Tomorrow you may learn the same thing about today…

- *The Lemonade:* The world is continuously improving, evolving, changing, and growing. If we don't keep up with it then we get carried backward. We need to be inquisitive and look forward to each day bringing new experiences, thoughts, feelings, emotions, and knowledge. Our learning should also be continuous, changing, and evolving. Every day you will be a better version of yourself. The love of life is the love of learning.

41. Approach situations with zest

"It is in the compelling zest of high adventure and of victory, and in creative action, that man finds his supreme joys." ~Antoine de Saint-Exupery

• *The Lemon:* Indifference, laziness, boredom, mindlessness. A truly apathetic lemon.

• *Ingredients:* Enthusiasm – for life. Creativity – try something new. Bravery – the courage to see what happens. Faith – the outcome will be good for you.

• *Preparation:* We can find zest or passion for so many things in our lives that are often approached with a mindless, routine attitude. Change your attitude, approach situations and activities with a keenness and gusto that says, "Wow, this is going to be fulfilling and worthwhile" and then it always will be. We provide great excuses. I don't have zest for this because I've been doing it every day for years and it's boring. Or, I don't have zest for this because I've never done it before and I don't know what to expect. First, if you keep doing what you've always been doing, you should expect the same result – boring. You create the boring. The boring isn't objective or intrinsic in the activity. It doesn't matter that you've been doing it for years. Make it new and exciting. Do it differently; learn something new about it; use your other (non-dominant) hand; teach someone how to do it; approach it like you will invent some new gadget that improves the efficiency or changes the process. Second, it might seem difficult at first is to be enthusiastic about trying new things. Don't just be willing to experiment with new activities and adventures. This negative hesitancy will occupy your thoughts, feelings, and emotions. They will take you away from the experience instead of having you completely involved. Rather, once you have committed to trying something new, accomplish it with zest, passion, and optimism. The whole event or activity will be more worthwhile and enjoyable. It will become a *flow* experience where time seems to standstill. You're in the zone!

• *The Lemonade:* If you exhibit zest, you will attract zest; and likeminded, positive people with zest. Zest begets zest. Happiness comes rarely from having things; it appears mostly when doing things that you enjoy with zest and enthusiasm. When you approach the world and life with zest, you bring an essential ingredient for happiness to the lemonade; intrinsic motivation. The doing becomes its own reward. Quite a satisfying lemonade!

42. Be honest with yourself and others

"Our lives improve only when we take chances - and the first and most difficult risk we can take is to be honest with ourselves."
~Walter Anderson

• *The Lemon:* Being dishonest and disingenuous to yourself and others. Insincere and deceitful. Trying or pretending to be something that you're not. You may fool others but it is harder to fool yourself.

• *Ingredients:* Kindness – to yourself and others. Integrity – moral and ethical. Truthfulness, Sincerity and Straightforwardness – genuine and authentic. Objective and Perspective – be detached when self-evaluating. Introspection – look inside before looking outside. Friends – what do they think?

• *Preparation:* I'm not just talking about *not* lying, *not* cheating, *not* stealing. Honesty involves positive virtues and actions; practicing kindness, integrity, and truthfulness. This precludes hedonism – honesty purely for improving your own pleasure, or honesty that is knowingly going to unnecessarily hurt others. Take time with yourself and objectively evaluate who you are. Be introspective – look at your goals, family, strengths, career, spirituality, desires, and weaknesses. No, perhaps you haven't won the Oscar or the Nobel Prize yet. Be kind to yourself; keep things in perspective. Find out from friends how they view you. What impression are you trying to give? What impression have you given? Notice that fear is left out of this recipe. Fear is what inspires people to lie, act deceitfully and be dishonest with themselves and others. Fear leads to repression and denial and is the biggest enemy of integrity. If fear gets in this lemonade it will cause a lot of clumping.

• *The Lemonade:* Be yourself – everyone else is already taken. Are you flying by the seat of your pants? Do you have plans for your life or things that you'd like to achieve? What are you waiting for? It's hard to make plans for yourself if you don't really know who you are. Being honest with yourself is the first step toward making introductions and establishing your personal path. Aligning your life journey with your truest values and ideals while using your best strengths to achieve them is a wonderful way to bring happiness and satisfaction to your life.

43. Take a nap

"No day is so bad it can't be fixed with a nap."

~Carrie Snow

• *The Lemon:* Being drowsy and not having the energy to pay attention to your job, your kids, your significant other, or other activities that would otherwise be more important.

• *Ingredients:* <u>18 to 25 minutes</u> – longer than this leads to grogginess. <u>Quite, Comfortable space</u> – no interruptions allowed. <u>Darken</u> the room. <u>Earplugs or White noise</u> – decrease chance of waking early. <u>Alarm</u> – decrease chance of sleeping late. <u>Self-confidence</u> – don't feel guilty about taking time for yourself. <u>Caffeine</u> – just a thought. <u>Meditation</u> – simulates a nap when you only have five minutes to relax.

• *Preparation:* Power naps are short periods of sleep that stop before the onset of deep sleep (or longer naps about 1 hour, that go all the way through the sleep cycle). After longer naps entering slow wave sleep but not completing the sleep cycle, you develop sleep inertia making you groggy and even harder to get going afterward. Brief naps revitalize and help make up for night-time sleep deficits. Power naps maximize sleep versus time while boost your performance. A twenty-minute power nap in the afternoon is better than sleeping twenty minutes longer in the morning. I'm not a coffee drinker or caffeine junkie but a caffeine nap – intake of caffeine prior to a short nap, has been shown to be a very effective way of decreasing driving accidents and sleepiness.

• *The Lemonade:* Taking naps three times per week may lower the chances of heart-related death. Naps are also beneficial for blood pressure control, diabetes, stroke, and weight gain. Just knowing that a nap is coming soon, has been shown to lower blood pressure. Napping for just twenty minutes can rejuvenate and refresh your mind and your body. It will boost your mood, lower your stress, and give you an energy and alertness kick that will improve your productivity. For performing some memory tasks, power naps may be as good as a full night of sleep. Naps make you smarter, safer and healthier – and all you have to do is relax – what a deal!

44. Say "I can" more than "I can't"

"It's kind of fun to do the impossible." ～Walt Disney

"When it comes to the future, there are three kinds of people: those who let it happen, those who make it happen, and those who wonder what happened."
～John M. Richardson

• *The Lemon:* Self-doubt. Fear. Repressing desires and dreams. Lack of hope or faith.

• *Ingredients:* <u>Dream</u> – what are the possibilities? <u>Faith</u> and <u>Confidence</u> – to do what you aren't *sure* that you can do. <u>Bravery</u> – to push beyond your comfort zone. <u>Curiosity</u> – to find out your potential. <u>Fortitude and Persistence</u> – anyone can give up, you have the potential to overcome.

• *Preparation:* To accomplish and achieve you must begin with a dream before you can do and act; this takes faith, confidence, and belief in yourself. Add to this the curiosity of finding out more about you and what you *can* do. Don't be persuaded by others who don't fully appreciate your potential or your drive. It's easy to quit and it's easier to not start on an unclear, untested path. Be persistent and have the fortitude to see it through. When you are trying to change a habit, don't keep it a secret; let others know. Telling friends and coworkers "I can quit smoking", "...drinking", "...showing up late", "I can resist those..." is much more effective in terms of you following through once you advertise it, than if you keep it to yourself.

Saying "I can" helps you dispel your own doubts and fears about whether you can accomplish a change.

- *The Lemonade:* I think I can, I think I can...this doesn't just apply to little engines. You will grow as high as you can reach, you will wander as far as you allow yourself to go, you will see as much as you open yourself up to seeing. Everyone is busy. We're all too busy to take on new tasks and activities and hobbies. So, if you want someone to do you a favor, who will most likely get the job done? The busiest person that you know. That's the person who has learned to take some of the brief moments of the day and expand them into valuable minutes. They start with the premise, "I can" do this. Don't push yourself beyond what is healthy for you to take on, but most of us waste so much time during the day, that as my daughter, Sarena has written, "Waste your time wisely." You may not know what you *can* do but if it's something that you want to accomplish, don't be limited by the fear of failure. Starting with "I can" statements is empowering and freeing.

45. *Assume there's something you don't know*

"It ain't what you don't know that gets you into trouble. It's what you know for sure that just ain't so."

~Mark Twain

• *The Lemon:* Being self-assured and cocky. Believing that you always know "the rest of the story". Becoming unnecessarily frustrated, disappointed, or angry at something or someone for failing to reach your expectations.

• *Ingredients:* <u>Humility</u> – No one can know everything. <u>Wisdom</u> – to know that you don't know. <u>Patience</u> – to find out more information. <u>Trust</u> and <u>Belief</u> - in others. <u>Open-minded</u> – there are usually many other possibilities.

• *Preparation:* When you are confused, angry, frustrated, and especially disappointed in something or someone, assume that you don't understand the complete picture. There is some vital piece of information that you are missing to complete the puzzle. ALWAYS. Even when it seems entirely obvious that you know all of the details, you very well may not. Start with this premise and then add the important principle that people are not out to get you. The world is not against you. Before you assume the worst by pretending that you know everything that there is to know about a given situation, be open-minded to the power of possibilities. There may be something that you heard incorrectly, mis-information; wrong time, day, month, person, or place. The only thing that you should ever assume is that without Paul Harvey, you won't know the rest of the story.

- *The Lemonade:* I've had a great education. Gone to school for dozens of years and to this day I take classes on a variety of topics. But the number of things that I don't know is extraordinary. I can't even begin to tell you simple things that go on in my daily life for which I don't know the full reason. When you start with the assumption that it is you that needs to find out more information to make a conclusion, your stress and frustration level will immediately decrease. You will be able to relax and inquisitiveness will replace anger. This state of mind will also facilitate your learning and increase your ability to form closer relationships with family, friends, and coworkers.

46. *Value your marriage*

"Happy marriages begin when we marry the ones we love, and they blossom when we love the ones we marry." Tom Mullen

- *The Lemon:* Poorly valued marriages result in unhappiness, lack of fulfillment, discontent, poor communication, disrespect, conflict, and eventually divorce. Groucho Marx said, "Marriage is a wonderful institution...but who wants to live in an institution?" These are not the values to which we espouse (or that we want our spouse to espouse).

- *Ingredients:* Friendship – best friends. Passion – friendship alone isn't enough. Love – is a many splendored thing. Compassion – more than just passion. Respect and Trust – necessary components in any relationship. Serenity and Comfort – taking time off from the passion.

- *Preparation:* Learning to value your marriage is critical to fostering a close relationship with your spouse. Develop a healthy balance of being best friends and passionate lovers. How to achieve this? Surprise your spouse often and make regular time for just the two of you. Say, "I love you" every day, even if you don't feel like it sometimes. Don't speak badly about your marriage or spouse – even with your closest friends or family (except with a qualified counselor), and learn to get over the insignificant things that bother you. Instead, focus on your spouse's values, strengths, and virtues that you respect and love. You are never done working on your marriage.

• *The Lemonade:* Marriage is not an institution; it isn't even a noun. It is an ongoing process; a verb. We need to be continually practice marriaging. As individuals we each continually change and evolve. With both partners changing, so will our relationships. But boy is it worth working on. Your kids will be more likely to attend college and succeed academically; they'll be physically and emotionally healthier, less likely to abuse drugs or alcohol, less likely to commit delinquent behaviors, have better relationships and decreased chance of future divorce. For the couple, better marriages also result in improved physical and emotional health, greater wealth, better relationships with your kids, and greater life satisfaction. For communities this means lower crime rates, higher rates of home ownership, and healthier and more educated citizens. Talk about your win-win situation. Studies show that marriage is a more significant happiness factor than job satisfaction, money or community. Make marriage a priority and make sure that your spouse understands how important it is to you.

47. Say "yes" more than "no"

"The big question is whether you are going to be able to say a hearty yes to your adventure." ~ Joseph Campbell

- *The Lemon:* Being a "No man". Focusing on negativity and pessimism. A friend or family member asks a question or a stranger asks for your help and as soon as they start speaking you are getting ready to answer, "No". Often, you don't even let them finish asking the question before you interrupt with a horizontal shake of your head.

- *Ingredients:* Openness – who knows what you might try. Bravery – going where you've never been before. Curiosity – don't just be curious about what you'll find, but be curious as to how well you'll accomplish any task. Trust – in other people and in yourself.

- *Preparation:* Don't say, "Yes" out of fear or ease to please. Don't say, "Yes" when it goes against your principles or is unnecessarily dangerous or is potentially harmful to others. Instead, say "Yes" to open yourself up to new events, activities, people, sights and places. Where "no" is confining, restrictive and safe; "yes" unlocks, empowers and takes risks. "No" begins with a negative feeling before becoming a negative thought and transitioning to a negative word and lack of action. In contrast, "Yes" is initiated with an open mind and a background in optimism and trust. A positive feeling leading to a positive thought and resulting in positive language and behavior.

- *The Lemonade:*   Being a "Yes" man (aka Jim Carey). Reflexly saying, "Yes". Yes to opportunities, yes to requests, yes to invitations. Seize the occasion - Carpe diem. More frequently saying yes will open you up to new friendships while strengthening your existing relationships. You'll be perceived as being more approachable. You'll find yourself being more giving and altruistic. You will find yourself teaching more, learning more, and having more fun doing both of them. The increase in your spontaneity will bring you to places (both literally and figuratively) that you never dreamed of. As Dr. Seuss said, "And will you succeed? Yes indeed, yes indeed! Ninety-eight and three-quarters percent guaranteed!"

Making Lemonade

SOUPS AND *SALADS*

48. Enjoy the journey - there are no failures

"I didn't fail the test, I just found 100 ways to do it wrong."
~Benjamin Franklin

"I have not failed. I've just found 10,000 ways that won't work."
~Thomas Edison

• *The Lemon:* Viewing yourself as a failure. Being fooled into believing that challenges were really problems. Believing that you know the beginning and end of your journey and that if your expectations aren't realized, that you have failed.

• *Ingredients:* <u>Drive</u>, <u>Motivation</u> and <u>Resilience</u> – to continue the journey despite challenges. <u>Flexibility</u> – the path may change. <u>Curiosity</u> – interest that keeps you going during the changes. <u>Bravery</u> and <u>Courage</u> – to continue the journey into unchartered territories. <u>Mindfulness</u> – appreciating the process.

• *Preparation:* Failure is subjective. If you feel that after a given process, activity or journey, you attained nothing, accomplished nothing, and gained nothing or you quit part way, then you indeed failed. Fear limits us and may cause us to even fail to try; this is true failure. There are no bad journeys. Every journey is valuable and we may learn from every activity in which we are involved. To participate and not learn is to waste time. The goal isn't the summit; the goal is the journey to the summit. If someone flew you to the mountaintop, it would be a nice view but you would be missing the experience of the climb. If you climbed the mountain and didn't make it to the summit;

you would still have gained experience to make this worthwhile. The knowledge that you would have gained and the sights that you would have seen on the way will help you and others perform better and train better in the future.

• *The Lemonade:* Appreciating the journey and appreciating the unpredictability of the pathway. Knowing that when you follow your heart and are true to who you are, that is *your* right path. Understand how much you have benefited, learned and grown from the experiences. The history of most important discoveries is the story of success in the midst of what some might have considered failure. Taking detours and altering your life journey based on ongoing analysis of your strengths, virtues, values, and desires is not failure but the path of flexibility and wisdom. It is also the path to happiness and satisfaction.

49. Empathize

"If your emotional abilities aren't in hand...if you can't have empathy and have effective relationships, then no matter how smart you are, you are not going to get very far."   ~Daniel Goleman

• The *Lemon:* Alexithymia – means not understanding emotions in oneself; the first step to being able to empathize with others. Having very low social and emotional intelligence. Not being able to relate to other people in an emotional way. Being able to walk in someone else's shoes is a foreign concept. Being isolated and apathetic.

• *Ingredients:* Psychological air – listening with empathy (Stephen Covey). Compassion, Care and Concern – for others. Mindfulness – attention and alertness; a focus on the present. Intention – the intention is to grow and learn; not to help others as this causes a transition into sympathy. Emotional Intelligence – assess, identify, manage, and control the emotions of yourself and others.

• *Preparation:* To truly share another person's emotions and feelings. Not to sympathize and feel badly or sorry for someone. This is why empathy can occur without the use of compassion or concern or caring; however, I like to add these in for a better tasting lemonade. The ability to know, understand and relate to what others' are feeling, requires that you pay close attention to non-verbal communication and cues such as body language and facial expressions.

• *The Lemonade:* Being able to relate to the emotions, beliefs and desires of others. One of the great gifts of human beings is the ability to empathize. Research has shown that even children (7-12 years old) are naturally inclined to empathize for those in pain. During this time, areas of their brain involved in moral reasoning were activated. Empathy is an active process contributing to our growth, development, and the establishment of close relationships. An empathetic lemonade will greatly improve your emotional health and well-being as well as enhance your hope for the future as an agent of change.

50. Find Excuses for Others

"The real man is one who always finds excuses for others, but never excuses himself." ~ Henry Ward Beecher

• *The Lemon:* Blaming. Accusing. Finding fault in the smallest things that other people do that upset, frustrate or disappoint you. Lack of patience and jumping to conclusions increases your stress and harms your relationships.

• *Ingredients:* Patience – take a breath before you react. Curious and Open-minded – about why something may have occurred. Creative - to derive excuses for others. Respect for and Faith in –other people.

• *Preparation:* Find a way to make excuses for others and justify behavior that would otherwise frustrate or disappoint you. When you find yourself getting upset, disappointed or angry at something or someone, don't immediately react. Take a breath and try to relax. Be open-minded about various possibilities for why this occurred. Begin with the premise that people are good. Try giving someone the same excuse that you have used in the past for yourself when you did the same thing. When we do something "bad", we quickly come up with an excuse that blames some external factor (my boss, my kid's school, the babysitter, etc.). When someone else does something "bad" we quickly blame their personality and character, even if we don't know them - internal factors. This is the fundamental error of attribution. To change this, give someone the same external excuse that you would have given to yourself. Try to make it realistic and believe in it. Externalize!

- *The Lemonade:* Jumping to an external excuse for someone instead of a conclusion and a blame. Excuse and explain instead of accuse and complain. It will seem like a form of meditation in the rapidity with which you can relax after an apparent misdeed or mistake. When you are able to excuse others for minor infractions, you will be relaxed and approachable at times that you would normally be closed off and not listening. You will reduce your frustration and stress, enhance your happiness, and be able to form better and more meaningful relationships.

51. Judge favorably

"When you judge another, you do not define them, you define yourself. " ~Wayne Dyer

• *The Lemon:* Judging others harshly, with a presumption of guilt and an overriding sense of negativity and superiority.

• *Ingredients:* Open-mindedness – unassuming and unbiased, Faith and Trust – in the goodness of other people and of human nature. Presumption – of innocence. Kindness – treat everyone with goodwill. Fairness – respect for equity. Sympathy – compassion for others.

• *Preparation:* Use some of the excuses that you came up with in the last chapter to help you judge favorably. When you are not sure why someone did something, assume that it was for a good and positive intent. Even if you are wrong, you'll feel better and treat them better. Give the benefit of the doubt; this is one of the commandments in the Jewish faith. Mindfulness involves a detachment and non-judgmental attitude. If possible, go beyond detachment and not judging to the positive side of the equation. If you are not able to accomplish this, you should still keep the judgment to yourself and not further harm someone (they can succeed at this on their own). This is not to say that we should excuse reprehensible or harmful behavior. If this is a behavior or action that you feel should not persist, effect a change. But if you choose not to try to change it or when you are not sure about intentions, you should assume and assign positive motives to judge on the favorable side. Use sympathetic eyes. Innocent until proven guilty should not reside solely in our legal system – it's a take home message as well.

• *The Lemonade:* When you don't know the reason behind something, assume that it happened for a good reason. What irritates us about others is often what we are lacking in ourselves. While this may start as a gift to someone else, it will quickly transform into a gift for you as you will benefit from this altruistic attitude. You will also be more relaxed, less stressed, frustrated, and angry. This will positively affect everything else that goes on in your day. Judging others is a reflection of how we judge ourselves. Putting others in a positive light will reflect on how you view yourself in a non-critical, optimistic, loving way – a clear path to a happy and satisfying life.

52. Practice loving-kindness meditation

"To love our enemy is impossible. The moment we understand our enemy, we feel compassion towards him/her, and he/she is no longer our enemy."

~ Thich Nhat Hanh

• *The Lemon:* Being uptight and stressed. Hateful and hurtful behavior. Disrespecting and criticizing others.

• *Ingredients:* Find a <u>Comfortable</u> location – you don't need to be isolated. <u>Self-acceptance</u> – before accepting others. <u>Gratefulness</u> – appreciating your gifts. <u>Empathy</u> – this is more important than sympathy.

• *Preparation:* Hatred and loving-kindness meditation (LKM) cannot coexist in the same mind. Choose LKM to increase empathy and produce four qualities of love: friendliness, compassion, appreciative joy and equanimity. LKM begins with loving acceptance of oneself, then moves to loving acceptance to others: 1) respected figure, 2) close family member or friend, 3) neutral person, and 4) hostile person. Find a relaxing place (internally and externally) and use breathing exercises. Focus on realizing that everyone deserves to be respected and loved. Think of things that we take for granted and understand how all that we have and all that we are is due to the kindness and goodness of others. We were given the education, training, and opportunity to allow us to succeed. Appreciate and express this. Focus on how we have benefited from the compassion and kindness of others. Visualize yourself in a mirror or the person you are thinking of smiling back at you with true happiness. Concentrate specifically on the things for which you are grateful and the positive qualities of that person. You may want to repeat a mantra or chant about lovingkindness to maintain your focus. Concentrate on empathy rather than sympathy.

- *The Lemonade:* You will benefit immediately from changing your thought patterns in a positive way. LKM helps you remain kindhearted and caring toward everybody with a healthy balance of loving feelings and acceptance in all situations and relationships. We are all formed from the same materials and micro particles; and thus interconnected in many ways, including a web of kindness. Taking this to the streets and applying those same feelings to those who you interact with daily will enhance relationships with coworkers, friends, and family. It will leave you with a glow of serenity, peacefulness, and gratitude.

53. Don't believe in absolutes

"Dogmatism and skepticism are both, in a sense, absolute philosophies; one is certain of knowing, the other of not knowing. What philosophy should dissipate is certainty, whether of knowledge or ignorance." ~Bertrand Russell

• *The Lemon:* Believing in absolutes; that people or things can be absolutely good or bad. When you believe in absolutes, you deny other possibilities or alternative endings. When there is a change, your world collapses. Being limited to single perspective thinking. Whatever is true at one time, at one place, for one person is going to always be true in all places for all people.

• *Ingredients:* Knowledge – a clear understanding that while we may know the *truth*, we may not really know the absolute *Truth* (or there may not even be one). Open-minded – so many possibilities. Relativity – what are you comparing it to? Flexibility – the ability to change your mind (if you're not happy with the mind that you have). Self-confidence – to admit that you don't know.

• *Preparation:* Claiming to have absolute knowledge is stifling to creativity and the pursuit of learning. There are very few absolutes in this world. A snow-covered mountain is beautiful or horrible depending on whether you are skiing on it or trying to drive around it through traffic to get to the other side. A brisk rainfall is refreshing and nourishing for the garden or disastrous for your picnic. These are not good or bad – their value is context-sensitive and you supply the context (subjectivity). Bring a healthy amount of doubt; you can accept that lots of people know a truth, but doubt that anyone knows *the* Truth. Be open-minded to the possibility that things may be very different. Be flexible to the multitude of possibilities that await you once you decide that anything is possible. Everyone has a default setting of bias. Move beyond seeing the world through your own single perspective and appreciate the subjectivity of our assessments.

- *The Lemonade:* Believing in the power of possibility, the power of flexibility, the power of change, and the power of perspectives. Asking great questions in search of more information and not accepting the status quo. Being able to grow, learn, develop, build, and broaden your understanding. This will also lead you to the path of building and broadening your social base as you are viewed as being less rigid and more flexible.

54. Appreciate moments of joy, inspiration, & awe

"The most beautiful thing we can experience is the mysterious. It is the source of all true art and all science. He to whom this emotion is a stranger, who can no longer pause to wonder and stand rapt in awe, is as good as dead: his eyes are closed." ~Albert Einstein

- *The Lemon:* Apathy, boredom, contempt. Joyless indifference.

- *Ingredients:* Enthusiasm - embracing life. Gratitude – active appreciation. Reverence – allow yourself to feel honor and respect. Admiration and Respect – a high regard for people, places and things.

- *Preparation:* The Grand Canyon, the roar of a waterfall, the Great Pyramids, the Roman Coliseum, and the birth of our children are obvious awe inspiring sights. Try to enthusiastically expand this list to include more of the ordinary. Adding gratitude to the universe and our ability to experience these things to bring joy and awe into our daily life. Awe infers either more fearful or more respectful than wonder and joy. Forget the fear and focus on the respect and surprise. Don't just wait until you're on a once-in-a-lifetime vacation to be awed. Awe and wonder are not objective, built-in qualities; they are subjective and completely depend on your views and attitudes. Joy is everywhere around you just waiting for you to tap into it.

• *The Lemonade:* Finding the beauty in characteristics, qualities, behaviors, attitudes, sights, and events that others miss daily. Experience the overwhelming feelings of inspiration, admiration, elation and wonder. Awe can inspire a spiritual (not necessarily religious) feeling of reverence. Occurrences of wonder, joy and awe are directly related to either pleasure or satisfaction. When you learn to bring these sensations and feelings into all aspects of your life, everything becomes greatly valued and appreciated.

55. Actively listen

"Knowledge speaks, but wisdom listens." ~Jimi Hendrix

"Deep listening is miraculous for both listener and speaker. When someone receives us with open-hearted, non-judging, intensely interested listening, our spirits expand." ~Sue Patton Thoele

• *The Lemon:* Not listening attentively. When someone is speaking to you, instead of listening, you are either distracted, not paying attention or thinking about your response. You believe that you already know what the other person is going to say or how they feel and you turn off.

• *Ingredients:* Respect – don't just feel it, listen like you mean it. Empathy – feel what they feel. Self-confidence – to know that you might be wrong. Understanding – not just the words but the feelings and meanings. Questions – ask when you don't know. Mindfulness – listen to facial expressions and body language in addition to words. Eye Contact – important in non-verbal communication.

• *Preparation:* Active listening is a focused attempt to understand not simply what someone else is saying but what is the deeper meaning and what are they feeling. The words may only be 10% of the message. The other 90% is non-verbal and requires empathy and a deeper level of attention. Truly understanding, evaluating and interpreting what you have heard. When someone speaks to you, focus on them, not yourself. Do not judge. If your first thought is that you disagree with the concept or statement, ask for clarification; assume that there is something that you don't understand. Paraphrase and repeat the thought back to them and ask them if this is what they meant. Ask questions. Don't be defensive. Don't deny the other person's validity by diagnosing and judging. Focus on respect, empathy, and understanding.

• *The Lemonade:* Doctors, counselors, and psychologists while talking to patients use this form of communication. It ensures accuracy, decreases miscommunication, acknowledges caring and compassion and improves satisfaction. Active listening improves personal and professional relationships through reducing conflicts, strengthening cooperation, and fostering understanding. Creating an atmosphere of collaboration will enhance your appreciation for yourself and others. You'll get people to open up during conversations and build a sense of trust and caring.

56. *Want what you have*

"I have no money, no resources, no hopes. I am the happiest man alive. "   ~Henry Miller

• *The Lemon:* Focusing on getting what you want and never being satisfied. When you do get what you want, you find out that it wasn't really something that you wanted after all. Wow, you're hard to please. The sadness of continuously unfulfilled desires.

• *Ingredients:* <u>Compassion</u> – for what you already have. <u>Gratitude</u> and <u>Appreciation</u> – try to find new meanings in old things. <u>Attention</u> – being mindful of what you have and why you have them. <u>Self-control</u> – it's OK to stop wanting for a while. <u>Contentment</u> – more than pursuit.

• *Preparation:* Happiness doesn't come from having a bunch of things. Even if they were things that you really wanted at one point. Happiness comes from wanting the things that are in your possession. Keep your desires under control. Research shows that students who want more of what they have are happier than those who are less fond of their possessions. This doesn't mean that you shouldn't goal-set or have a list of places that you would like to go or things that you would like to own. But don't focus on "things" for their own sake – keeping up with the Joneses…Focus on what they will allow you to do in terms of activities that you would enjoy.

- *The Lemonade:* Happiness comes from wanting what you have; not having what you want. Getting what you want may result in brief periods of pleasure. However, we adapt and slowly return to our happiness set point – the pleasure dissipates. Instead, wanting and appreciating the things, people, and gifts with which we have been blessed, leads to long-term contentment and unbeatable satisfaction with life and all that it has to offer. Being happy for internal reasons rather than for external reasons; even good external reasons, means that your happiness is less dependent on circumstances and more dependent on your attitude which is completely under your control.

57. Acknowledge positive qualities

"Research has shown over and over again that the more you acknowledge your past successes, the more confident you become in taking on and successfully accomplishing new ones. You know that even if you fail, it won't destroy you, because your self-esteem is high." ~Jack Canfield

• *The Lemon:* Taking anything and everything for granted. Letting so many great things pass you by without giving them the attention that they deserve. Always focusing on improvement and not appreciating how great the thing is that is right in front of us.

• *Ingredients:* Appreciative Thoughts and Feelings – positive qualities are plentiful. Grateful – for the goodness surrounding you. Self-reflection – know who you are. Self-confidence – see the good in oneself.

• *Preparation:* Positive affirmations. Examples: "I am…", "I can…", "I do…", "You are getting a lot of chores done today." "You are a great chef", "You are a wonderful teacher." "I surprised myself by how well I could…", "I have conquered my fear of…" Positive qualities are found everywhere that we look and in everyone with whom we interact – feel it, think it, focus on it, say it, show it; don't keep it a secret. Look in the mirror and find positive qualities in the person staring back at you. Acknowledging is bringing positive focus and mindfulness to something that we appreciate. Be aware and appreciative of all of your positive skills, talents, and abilities: math and logic, music, visual, spatial, cooking, athletic, linguistic, communication, self-reflection, bravery, etc. Be aware of the same qualities in others. Let yourself know that you are aware of these; now let other people know that you are aware of their positive traits. Acknowledge at work, at home, at school, at the grocery store, or even when you're by yourself. Acknowledge in words, through letters or by deeds.

•   *The Lemonade:* Good stuff happens continuously. Acknowledging positivity brings it into the forefront of your attention and focus. It will bring out the best in you and the best in others. When everyone is at his or her best individually, our relationships are more fulfilling. Conflicts are resolved or forgotten and communication is improved. Opportunities to acknowledge the positive qualities of others will always strengthen bonds. Being aware of the goodness in our lives is a wonderfully rewarding and satisfying way to go through the day – looking forward to whatever comes your way. But acknowledging, rather than simply being aware of the positive, elevates us and moves us beyond feelings into the realm of action.

58. Hang with happy people

"Happy thoughts attract happy people into your life."
— Remez Sasson

• *The Lemon:* Negativity spirals. Interacting with negative people who help you on the downward vortex to further pessimism and harmful thoughts, feelings, words, and behaviors.

• *Ingredients:* Approachable – both the attitude and energy. Curiosity – increases your chance of being receptive to others. Trusting - A belief in the goodness of people. Smile – even just a little. Eye Contact – look up and look like you care. Body Language – emotional availability.

• *Preparation:* Emotions are infectious, so spend your free time with positive, optimistic people. You will find it difficult to attract happy people as friends if you aren't positive yourself. You need to do your part in the relationship. Be approachable; this means not being preoccupied or self-absorbed. Being curious and receptive increases the chances of attracting positive people. Just as you know which people are safe and easy to approach, everyone also knows this about you. Make it easy for them. A sincere smiling lets others know that they can at least relax around you. Use eye contact to let them know that you see them and that you care. Watch your body language. Avoid folding your arms across your chest, turning away from someone, looking at or texting on your cell phone, or other signals that say, "Don't come near me". Instead keep your hands open, plant your feet forward, face someone straight on with a calm, friendly and accepting look. Prioritizing anyone around you over your cell phone will always win you points in the relationship game. And while we're at it – unplug your headphones. When you are hanging with the happy, make sure that you nurture these relationships by showing gratitude, acknowledging their friendship, and displaying positive character traits so that they also want to hang around you.

- *The Lemonade:* Friends are great. Angry, frustrated or depressed friends increase our negative feelings; while happy, positive people perpetuate our propensity to positivity (sorry, couldn't help myself). No one is *always* happy, but finding people with a propensity to see the glass half full is a sure-fire way of improving your own happiness.

59. Create a Humor Depot

"...If you can make a girl laugh - you can make her do anything..."
~ Marilyn Monroe

• *The Lemon:* Laughter deficiency. Really sour lemons. Sadness and despair. Being the one at a party saying, "I don't have any good jokes," or "I just can't tell a joke well."

• *Ingredients:* DVD's and Funny books - other daily sources of references. Funny friends – you know that you have them, Pen and paper – don't rely on your memory.

• *Preparation:* Make use of vital resources that might enhance your repertoire like movies and TV shows, comics, funny books, funny (looking) friends, etc. Don't rely on a fabulous memory (optional ingredient); write things down. This will help you keep jokes and funny stories organized and improve your recall in the future. Keep note cards with jokes on them to make it an easy reference. Before you go to a party look over a few humorous note cards or carry a few of these cards around with you in your purse or pocket to glance at as reminders. When something is frustrating, turn it into a Jay Leno monologue to laugh it away. Think of how Jay (or the other late night guy) would retell this story. Don't forget to use these sources to cheer you up when you're feeling blue. Keep a "You said this" list. Write down funny things that you hear people say. Especially your children. Keep them in a notebook and you can write down when and where they said it. Write down the funniest things that ever happened to you. You'll see that not all of these things were funny at the time. Use this list to cheer yourself up and now you've got more material to entertain friends. "How do you get to the Met?" "Practice, practice, practice." Being someone who makes others laugh may not come naturally or easy. But if you don't try it or practice it, it won't come at all!

- *The Lemonade:* Being the one at the party who everyone is hanging around. Having a humor repertoire of materials upon which you can rely. Having friends ask you, "How do you remember all of those jokes and stories?" Humor enhances trust and trust enhances cooperation and cooperation enhances openness and openness enhances social bonding and social bonding enhances happiness and happiness enhances...wow!

60. *Practice creative altruism*

"Every man must decide whether he will walk in the light of creative altruism or in the darkness of destructive selfishness."   ~Martin Luther King, Jr.

• *The Lemon:* Having and not giving. Being self-absorbed and self-centered. Better to receive than to give.

• *Ingredients:* <u>Generosity</u>, <u>Compassion</u>, and <u>Kindness</u> – they're absolute musts. <u>Prosocial attitude</u> – can't be a lone wolf and effectively practice altruism. <u>Creativity</u> – brings altruism to another level. <u>Time</u> – it will be worth every minute. <u>Energy</u> – it will be well worth the effort. <u>Spirit</u> – not essential, but will make the experience more worthwhile. <u>Money</u> – sometimes required, although much can be accomplished without this ingredient. <u>Rule</u> – a Golden One. Do unto others…

• *Preparation:* Direct your money, kindness and compassion in the form of generosity toward others. A blend of prosocial attitude and creativity will help guide you in how and where to lend a hand. There are thousands of ways that we can help preserve, protect or restore land, animals, people, or even societies. Money can't always buy happiness, but in this case donating money to those who have little, will provide you with a happiness boost as you help those in need. Similarly donating books, clothes, or furniture to the needy won't just help the needy. Clean instruments for a third world medical mission, volunteer in a local hospital or blood drive or immunization clinic, serve or cook at a food pantry, assist patrons of a homeless shelter, clean local parks, plant community trees, clean and reorganize after natural disasters, deliver holiday gifts to the needy, join a science team to save endangered species, etc, etc, etc. If none of these tickle your fancy, bring your values and utilize your strengths in an internet search to find alternative opportunities to help others.

• *The Lemonade:* While altruism appears to represent selflessness in the form of giving, it truly is a win-win situation in which we also receive health and wellness benefits. When you are altruistic, you get rewarded with a release of pleasure-related brain chemicals like dopamine, endorphins, and oxytocin into the bloodstream causing a feel-great, helper's high. It doesn't matter what you are giving; time, money, things, or advice. When you do it with the true spirit of helping others and not what will you get in return or on your return, only then will you be entitled to the amazing health and wellness benefits of altruism.

61. Understand the importance of teamwork

"The way a team plays as a whole determines its success. You may have the greatest bunch of individual stars in the world, but if they don't play together, the club won't be worth a dime." ~ *Babe Ruth*

"Individual commitment to a group effort that is what makes a team work, a company work, a society work, a civilization work." ~ *Vince Lombardi*

• *The Lemon:* All for one and one for one. A lone wolf. Not taking help or offering help. Believing that there is an I in teamwork. Not trusting or respecting others enough to work with them.

• *Ingredients:* Self-confidence – required to be able to have confidence in others. Praise, Appreciate and Trust – the skill of others. Strength – through unity. Vision and Hope – objectives for the future. Belief in a Greater Purpose – it's more than just for me. Communication, Coordination and Cohesion – work together.

• *Preparation:* "Team" is an abbreviation for Together Everyone Achieves More. Bring some self-confidence and self-esteem to the table. You need to have faith in yourself and your abilities to be able to trust in the goodwill and strengths in others. In a cyclical fashion, being in a good mood makes a person more likely to be involved in social activities and work in a group. In turn, working in a group and being involved in social activities will help get a person into a good mood. Realize how much more can be accomplished as a group compared to as an individual. To truly value this result, requires a belief in a greater good and purpose than simply the desires of an individual. It requires faith in your fellow teammates as well as hope for the greater good by everyone coming to work together.

- *The Lemonade:* Working together toward a common vision or accomplishing organizational objectives. Common people with a unifying strength attain exceptional results. Teamwork is a synergistic phenomena; $1 + 1 + 1 = 4$. Together we are better than the sum of the individuals. We are stronger, smarter, faster, taller, and more creative. Being social and engaging in healthy social contacts is essential to our survival and our happiness.

62. *Develop specific goals*

"A goal without a plan is just a wish." ~Larry Elder

"If you want to live a happy life, tie it to a goal, not to people or things." ~Albert Einstein

• *The Lemon:* Wandering aimlessly, goal-lessly, and without a specific purpose. No direction or plans.

• *Ingredients:* Positive anticipation – for the future; in other words, having hope. Purpose – long-term and short-term. Conscientiousness – to thoughtfully complete a task. Perseverance and Resilience – when the going gets tough… Planning – prepare and organize. Strengths – know them and use them. Timelines – be specific. Reason – raison d'être.

• *Preparation:* While extrinsic goals are about meeting others' expectations, intrinsic goals are associated with personal values and are more often associated with increased happiness and satisfaction. Once a goal is established, approach it with a "will not fail" attitude and do your best to not just complete the goal, but to accomplish it thoroughly and with a sense of purpose. View obstacles as challenges and situations. Goals should be thought of as one important step along a journey. Try hard to accomplish them, yet realize that the process is just as important (sometimes more important) than the outcome. Developing specific goals entails an assessment of your needs, wants, desires, values, and strengths. Potential challenges should be evaluated and attention should be paid to resources and the support necessary to overcome these challenges. Implicit in setting up goals are specific timelines to keep you on track. Without timelines, goals become vague "want to's". Before you undertake the goal, analyze and clearly delineate why this is important to you. If you aren't clear on this, you will lose your purpose, focus and drive at the first obstacle. The "why" is what will motivate you when you don't feel like continuing. Make material success a side-effect of an intrinsic goal that involves creating something or improving a product or service. Draw on your strengths and keep your fears and insecurities in check. Don't keep it a secret! Make an action plan and remember that you have to act to achieve, not just think about it. You're not just the producer of this play; you're the director and the lead actor.

• *The Lemonade:* Having a sense of purpose. Increasing success, satisfaction, and sense of accomplishment. Short-term goals continuously reinforce our self-confidence and self-trust that we can do what we say we will do. They also give us a chance to develop new skills or sharpen old ones. Long-term goals stimulate us to make dreams into a reality. They energize our hopes and help us organize our lives. Goals keep us motivated, excited, and appreciative.

63. Eliminate problems

"Opposition is a natural part of life. Just as we develop our physical muscles through overcoming opposition – such as lifting weights – we develop our character muscles by overcoming challenges and adversity."
~Stephen R. Covey

• *The Lemon:* Everything is a problem…and problems are bad. Problems invoke and promote fear, frustration, resentment, disappointment, and immobility. They prevent us from achieving and accomplishing our goals and dreams.

• *Ingredients:* Reframing - problems as challenges or perhaps even opportunities. Self-acceptance – for meeting challenges. Hope, Faith, Self-Confidence, and Courage – without these challenges and opportunities become problems.

• *Preparation:* You are more powerful than you even realize. Right now you have the power to alleviate all the problems in your life. It's true. With one attitudinal and cognitive change, your *problems* can transform into *issues, situations, challenges, or opportunities.* Having hope and faith that there is a greater good or purpose in your life or a belief in something greater than ourselves helps us make the transformation from problem to challenge. This transformation doesn't just change the problem; it changes us. Nobody looks forward to dealing with problems that would be masochistic; but getting the chance to overcoming challenges is exciting and a potentially positive experience.

Your growth and development depend on how you apply yourself to challenges; don't wait until everything is perfect – there is no perfect. Have the courage and self-confidence to look forward to challenges. See what you're made of and be proud of triumphing over your fears. The greater the challenge, the stronger, more courageous, more confident, and more successful you become.

• *The Lemonade:* Without accepting and facing challenges, you will never feel the exhilaration of conquering them. Facing challenges builds our faith, inner strength, and courage, which in turn energize us and boost our confidence and positive self-assessment. Successfully taking on a challenge, even unsuccessfully is empowering and liberating. So much so that you will find yourself actually looking forward to challenges; not to impress others (extrinsic motivation), but to continue your spiritual, emotional, intellectual, and physical journey of growth.

Making Lemonade

ENTREES

64. Believe in the importance of now

"Life is now. There was never a time when your life was not now, nor will there ever be." ~ Eckhart Tolle

• *The Lemon:* Focusing on the past and the future. Missing out on once-in-a-lifetime moments and experiences because you are only physically here, your mind, your thoughts, and your soul are elsewhere - you might as well be too!

• *Ingredients:* Attention and Awareness – mindfulness. Don't just be here; be here and aware. Focus – on the now. Redirection – your thoughts will wander, expect this, forgive this, don't dwell on this or blame yourself. Gently redirect your thoughts back to now. Trust – that now will be more rewarding than the past or future. Courage to stay in the present moment and not let your mind dream or wander.

• *Preparation:* Mindfulness is *this* and *here*. Living in the present moment. This requires your full attention and awareness – all the time. It also requires that you not compare anything to the here and now. As Baba Ram Dass has written, "Be Here Now". Indeed believing and practicing present living and accepting present moment reality is empowering. Don't daydream. Whatever activity you are involved in, including listening; give it your full, undivided attention. There is nothing more important than now or here. Stop comparing things, events and people. Heraclitus said that you cannot step twice into the same river because the river has flowed on; everything has changed. Indeed you have also flowed on; your thoughts, feelings, and emotions have changed and will continue to change. The changing, flowing river is not doing so every fifteen minutes. It is continuously in flux (as are you) and thus it is impossible to step in the same river even once. When your thoughts wander to the past and future, become softly aware of this and gently guide them back to the present moment. Forgive yourself.

• *The Lemonade:* There is nothing as fulfilling as the here and now. Full attention to other people will result in more profound, deeper, richer, and closer relationships and fewer conflicts. Full attention to activities and events will lead to greater satisfaction, enhanced performance and learning, greater safety, and improved concentration and enjoyment. Everything becomes more stimulating and edifying. Even mundane repetitive activities become exciting as you realize that they are not repetitive; you are different than you were yesterday so nothing can be the same. There is nothing permanent except change. Being fully present will bring you to a place of deep serenity and peace as well as a life full of intense aliveness, joy, awe, and appreciation.

65. *Focus on joy over pleasure*

"Pleasure is always derived from something outside of you, whereas joy arises from within." ~ Eckhart Tolle

"I sometimes wonder whether all pleasures are not substitutes for joy." ~ C.S. Lewis

• *The Lemon:* Transiently satisfying biological drives – eat, exercise, sex, and excretory functions. Seeking out external sources, such as recreational drug use to make you feel good. Choosing superficial pleasure over heart-felt joy. Pleasure (the absence of pain) – not a great path to lasting fulfillment.

• *Ingredients:* Surprise – unexpected moments of positivity. Enthusiasm – for something greater. Reverence and Appreciation – for a more meaningful version of happy. Self-control – don't always go for the easy pleasure. Wisdom – to know the difference between joy and pleasure. Moderation – resisting some temptations.

• *Preparation:* Pleasure is a fleeting feeling that often involves things happening to us. It narrows our focus to the object of desire and depends on circumstances that can quickly disappear. You can have more pleasurable than non-pleasurable experiences, yet at the end of the day your overall feeling may be quite negative. Joy opens our minds to possibilities and stimulates our creative juices (lemonades). Be enthusiastic about involving joy in your life and appreciate the significant amount of long-lasting positivity that experiencing joy can bring.

Understand that sometimes the difference between pleasure and joy is all in the attitude. Having sex can fulfill bodily desires and bring pleasure or having sex with your spouse may bring you joy if your focus is on deeper feelings of love. Similarly, eating a great meal - pleasurable, eating a great meal that your children cooked for you involves pride and gratitude – joy. Here is the secret. Every great meal was cooked by someone and the food was from somewhere (God, the universe, Mother Nature), somehow you are privileged enough to be here now eating it and have the senses necessary to fully appreciate it. Use these thoughts to bring gratitude, hope, faith, inspiration, interest, and awe to the experience and you will transform pleasure into joy.

• *The Lemonade:* When pleasurable needs are satisfied, the pleasure may actually transform into something negative like revulsion; like too much food or sex. Joy, on the other hand, fuels a creative and/or playful urge. When you are experiencing joy, colors are brighter, the room is lighter, your aches and pain disappear, everyone is friendlier and there are fewer strangers. You feel younger, more alive and satisfied with life and your life circumstances. Unlike pleasure, which may briefly enhance your subjective well being, the joy effects are long lasting and heart-felt.

66. *Believe in something greater than yourself*

"We are not human beings on a spiritual journey. We are spiritual beings on a human journey."
~Dr. Stephen Covey

"This is my simple religion. There is no need for temples; no need for complicated philosophy. Our own brain, our own heart is our temple; the philosophy is kindness."
~The Dalai Lama

• *The Lemon:* Believing that there is no purpose to this life. No God, no Buddha, no Allah, no Jesus. We are here alone with no pathway or journey. Spiritual hunger can't be satisfied at McDonalds or by more credit card purchases.

• *Ingredients:* Faith – that everything is as it should be. Purpose – you are here for a reason. Hope and Trust – in something or some process. Awe and Inspiration – for the greatness and beauty that is all around you. Belief – in what you can only feel.

• *Preparation:* Most people don't know that they're on a spiritual path; it is simply our life journey. We may be programmed with a "God gene" or neurochemically wired to believe in a higher power or it may be preordained to help us unite with a life-giving, life-sustaining energy or with the Almighty. You can call it God, Jesus, Allah, Shiva, Mother Nature, Universal Phlegm, or a Sacred Journey. Believe in some force, someone or some process which will keep you on the right spiritual path while helping you keep faith, hope, gratitude, forgiveness, awe, inspiration, and love at the forefront of your decisions and actions. Believe in a greater good – that's why you are here; your purpose. A belief in helping others is a greater good that will guide and direct you. This spiritual feeling can involve, but does not require religious observance. Nature may hold the key to your intellectual and spiritual satisfaction. Simply attending religious services without a true belief or practice of what is preached will not provide you with the spiritual fuel or benefits that you will reap when you believe spiritually not ritualistically.

- *The Lemonade:* There is a reason that spirituality is at the top of Maslow's Hierarchy of Needs. When your thoughts, feelings, emotions, attitudes, and behaviors have positive spiritual tour guides. It's like having a rudder on your ship to keep you in better alignment with prevailing winds so that you don't go too far off course. From these beliefs come serenity and peace, determination and motivation, resilience, fortitude and tolerance, gratitude and forgiveness, altruism, compassion, and respect for all; a reverence for life that keeps us fulfilled, invigorated, and with a sense of awe. Religious involvement in adults predicts well-being, and happiness and may provide an excellent means of social support. Spiritual people are also physically healthier, get sick less often, are less stressed, and even live longer. So what's so bad about that?

67. *Negate negatives* (adapted from Dr. Martin Seligman)

"People who project negativity typically have low self-esteem. They feel badly about themselves, and their negativity is simply a reflection of those feelings."

~Hendrie Weisinger

"Aggressive fighting for the right is the noblest sport the world affords." ~Theodore Roosevelt

• *The Lemon:* Thinking negative things about oneself and hearing the same comments from others...and believing them. Obesity, suicide, low intelligence, heart attacks, strokes, eating disorders, violence, depression – need I say more?

• *Ingredients:* <u>Awareness</u> – identify negativity in your thoughts and others' words. <u>Beliefs</u> – if the negative thoughts were true, what are the consequences? <u>Dispute</u> – argue with yourself. <u>Self-confidence</u> – appreciate you and stand up for what is right.

• *Preparation:* Negative thoughts won't all vanish. Even optimistic people will have negative thoughts. If someone said to you, "You are really stupid," you would instantly come up with several arguments and valid reasons why that person is wrong. Yet, when you make a mistake and tell yourself that you are stupid, you believe it. Believing that internal voice will lead to pessimism, insecurity, self-doubt, anxiety, depression, and anger. Argue with yourself when you go to the negative; don't just ignore it because it will still be there. Dispute negative thoughts.

Give specific details about how this is wrong and now look at how much better you feel. When you encounter a person making a negative comment about a third party, don't just listen and disagree in your thoughts and feelings. Stand up for them and for what is right. You can put an end to negative spiraling. Don't pass on negative rumors, dispute them and be proud of yourself that you did. Affirmations instead of ruminations.

- *The Lemonade:* Changing the way you view yourself is the first step to changing how we view the world. Negating your own negatives is like getting a shot of adrenaline-charged lemonade. It is an empowering technique to bring more positivity into your life, enhance your subjective well-being, and improve your self-acceptance and sense of self-worth. Disputing negative comments by others will also put you in a powerful position to creating an air of goodwill, friendship, cooperation, and compassion.

68. *Perpetuate positives*

"Few things in the world are more powerful than a positive push. A smile. A word of optimism and hope. And you can do it when things are tough."
~ Richard M. DeVos

"Enter every activity without giving mental recognition to the possibility of defeat. Concentrate on your strengths, instead of your weaknesses...on your powers, instead of your problems."
~ Paul J, Meyer

• *The Lemon:* Focusing on negatives. Being gloomy, pessimistic, and unpleasant. Passing on destructive rumors. Being actively disengaged at work. Complaining and blaming friends, family, and coworkers.

• *Ingredients:* Playful – sometimes look at the silly side of life. Creativity – to bring positive comments into a negative conversation. Gratitude and Appreciation – lots of people to thank. Interest – in what's going on around you. Respect and Kindness – for others even when they are not present. Patience and Fortitude – this may not be taken well by others at first.

• *Preparation:* You're in a group and someone's name comes up in conversation. Be the first to say something nice. If something negative is said about them, mention something on their behalf. If you have nothing good to say, change topics. If you are starting a conversation, begin with a positive remark about the weather, your day or about the person you are speaking with. When you hear something positive said or you witness a positive event, follow through and enhance the positives. Try to come up with innovative ways to compliment, show gratitude, praise, or give accolades. Your friends and family may not appreciate you continually pointing out "the bright side" of things, so be patient. Once they feel the upward spiral, they will also be sucked in (in a good way).

- *The Lemonade:* Positivity feels good. The more you are involved with it the better it feels. It will expand your thoughts and your mind, inspires creativity, innovation, openness, and compassion. Perpetuating positives will help you build vital intellectual, physical, emotional, and spiritual resources. The increase in your potential is exponential. That means that once you get to a certain point, the results are nonlinear; putting a little in, brings about extraordinary benefits in outcome. This is a great technique for building social ties and forging closer relationships.

69. *Change your self-explanatory style* (adapted from Dr. Martin Seligman)

"A pessimist sees the difficulty in every opportunity; an optimistic sees the opportunity in every difficulty."
~ Winston Churchill

"The optimist proclaims that we live in the best of all possible worlds. The pessimist fears this is true."
~ James Branch Cabell

• *The Lemon:* Blaming ourselves for negatives. Generalizing negative events as representative of everything else in our lives and believing it will be like this forever. Positive events happen because I was lucky or someone else made them happen. Positive feelings are fleeting and limited in their impact. What a pessimistic lemon – Yuck!

• *Ingredients:* Hope – for the future. Faith – in positive outcomes. Self-confidence – a strong sense of self-worth. Self-control – place limits on your negative self-assessments. Disputes – argue with yourself when you start to use a pessimistic style.

• *Preparation:* Look at how you explain things to yourself when positive or negative events happen. Use a positive explanatory style to focus on the permanent and pervasive aspects of any event. Permanence: View positive things as lasting a long time ("I always find my way"), while negative events are transient and brief ("I'm sure I'll do better on tomorrow's test). Pervasive: The situation affects all aspects of your life. Positive situations should be generalized ("Everything I touch turns to gold"), while negatives should be limited in significance ("I didn't do well on a small assignment at work, but the sales meeting went great"). Using a positive or optimistic explanatory style you are more likely to take credit for good events while blaming others for negative situations. This is the only section of the explanatory style that I don't recommend – rather than blaming others, you can still take responsibility without feeling negative and blaming yourself.

- *The Lemonade:* Positive experiences are optimistically-labeled as internal, stable, and global. Your attributional style is closely related to your degree of optimism. Sales people who have an optimistic explanatory style have been shown to be more resilient. Others with an optimistic style felt they had more control of their health and were less at risk of getting sick. Pessimistic styles, on the other hand, may be associated with depression and physical illnesses.

70. *Develop your signature (strengths*) (adapted from Dr. Chris Peterson).

"Hide not your talents. They for use were made. What's a sundial in the shade." ~Benjamin Franklin

"Success is achieved by developing our strengths, not by eliminating our weaknesses." ~Marilyn vos Savant

- *The Lemon:* Not knowing what you are doing with your life. Questioning if you are in the right job and about choices in your personal life. Not having a sense of your talents, virtues, and strengths.

- *Ingredients:* <u>Self-awareness</u> – to understand you. <u>Curiosity</u> – to really investigate who you are. <u>Self-worth</u>, <u>Dedication</u> and <u>Fortitude</u> – to perform at your peak. <u>Computer</u> – to go online and figure out your strengths.

- *Preparation:* Distinguish your natural talent from what you can learn and identify your dominant talents. Synergy occurs when your strengths are well applied and matched to the job needs and the work of the organization. Finding positions where your weaknesses are not a major component of your daily work will help lower our stress and enhance our performance. Positive psychology has delineated seven virtues: wisdom and knowledge, courage, humanity, justice, temperance, and transcendence. Each virtue has several strengths. You can find out your top (signature strengths at www.viacharacter.org. or at www.strengthfinder.com. Rather than trying to improve all of your weaknesses, focus on developing and using your strengths. There are five character strengths that are highly associated with life satisfaction: love, hope, gratitude, curiosity, and zest.

- *The Lemonade:* Understanding and utilizing one's strengths are critical to both your success and satisfaction in life. Matching your personal strengths to your work and hobbies, helps you live a life of value. You will work and play with a passion and compassion that will be contagious. You have more strength in you than you ever dreamed of. There will be more intrinsic motivation in your work and you will be less reliant on external motivational factors (although you will receive more external praise because of your improved work ethic, commitment, and dedication).

71. *Best possible selves* (Adapted from Dr. Sonja Lyubomirsky)

"All men are sculptors, constantly chipping away the unwanted parts of their lives, trying to create their idea of a masterpiece." ~Eddie Murphy

"There is nothing noble about being superior to some other person. The true nobility is in being superior to your previous self." ~Hindustani Proverb

• *The Lemon:* Having a depressing view about what your future will look like and having a poor self-image; not being able to look to the future with hope. Seeing no need for self-improvement or growth – being satisfied with the status quo.

• *Ingredients:* Self-awareness and Social intelligence – who are you now and what are your strengths and values? Hopes, Dreams and Aspirations – who do you want to be? Creativity and Imagination – your choices are enormous. Self-confidence and self-worth – you have so many opportunities. Significant Others – get positive feedback. Pen and Paper – don't keep it in your head.

• *Preparation:* Think about your future. Imagine and visualize that everything has gone as well as it possibly could; you have achieved everything that you've wanted. Think about how you would look and feel? What would you be doing? What could you see yourself doing that would make you most proud? This will require some insight into your emotions, motives, values, and goals. Don't just think about this, write it down to help you organize your thoughts and feelings. Now go out and recruit a few friends and get some positive feedback from them. Make sure they know that you're not just looking for compliments. Perhaps try to get them involved in doing the same exercise. Synthesize their comments with yours into a representation of your "best self". Write for 20 minutes per day for three or four days in a row. You will develop strategies on how to get where you want to be. Writing forces our brain to be structured, intentional, and organized. Those who set goals and have a good attitude about getting there set in motion self-fulfilling prophecies.

• *The Lemonade:* Writing about your best possible future enhances insight into your emotions, motives, values, and goals. You will meld your life experiences and values into a framework upon which to future focus. It will provide you with a feeling of control over your destiny and help you envision a specific and more concrete pathway to fulfill your goals. This will empower you with an energetic burst of lemonade that will improve your performance, enhance your psychological well-being, and even make you happier.

72. Look for blessings in disguise

"What seems to us as bitter trials are often blessings in disguise." ~Oscar Wilde

"Our real blessings often appear to us in the shape of pains, losses and disappointments." ~Joseph Addison

- *The Lemon:* Accepting life's apparent negatives as being truly bad. Not appreciating that providence may create situations that are exactly what you need, but not know it.

- *Ingredients:* <u>Assumption</u> and <u>Belief</u> – that there will always be a blessing. <u>Hope</u>, <u>Faith</u> and <u>Trust</u> – that the world (God, Mother Nature, the Universe) gives you gifts and that things will work out well in the end. <u>Enthusiasm</u> and <u>Zest</u> – to discover the blessing, embrace life and find the gift. <u>Gratitude</u> – use this to replace the blaming and other negative emotions. <u>Creativity</u> and <u>Curiosity</u> – to find the blessing.

- *Preparation:* Start with a basic assumption and a belief that there is a blessing that may not be readily apparent at first or second glance. You'll need hope, faith, and trust that there is a purpose to your journey here on earth and that you will benefit from this incident or event. Be interested and inspired to discover the blessing and keep an open mind as to how this apparent negative will, in the end, be a blessing. Don't assume the worst. Try to approach apparently negative situations with enthusiasm and gratitude rather than with fear and blame.

- *The Lemonade:*   Realizing and appreciating that behind apparent negatives are typically disguised blessings. Sometimes these blessings are very well disguised; but be rest assured that they are still there. Don't wait until the blessing is revealed. You will reap the benefits of reduced frustration, disappointment, and stress if your first reaction is at least the question, "How will this be good?" As I described in the introduction, I was diagnosed with glaucoma and stated on treatment following an unrelated eye injury. There are hundreds of personal examples of blessings. We all have blessings; it's up to you to recognize and make the best use of them. Don't miss an incredible opportunity to grow, learn and develop because you are too busy being self-absorbed with "Why did this happen to me?"

73. *3 good things* *(adapted from Dr. Martin Seligman)*

"Life is full of beauty. Notice it. Notice the bumble bee, the small child, and the smiling faces. Smell the rain, and feel the wind. Live your life to the fullest potential, and fight for your dreams." ~Ashley Smith

• *The Lemon:* Not appreciating how incredible your life is. Waiting for amazing, awe-inspiring events and missing out on all of the great things that are continually going on.

• *Ingredients:* Appreciation – for anything good. Memory – for little positive events. Self-reflection – what was your role? Fortitude – don't give up this exercise. Pen and Paper – write them down.

• *Preparation:* Each night before you go to sleep, reflect on your day and come up with three good things that happened to you or with you during the day. These don't have to be (and in fact, shouldn't be) amazing things; anything that you would consider positive – a nice dinner, encountering an old friend, hearing some good news about someone, etc. Write down the three good things and with each one, reflect on why they happened and what your role was. The nice dinner may have occurred because your significant other took the time to go shopping and find a new recipe to try that included some of your favorite ingredients. This last step is very important to help you appreciate and find gratitude for others and to improve your sense of self-worth and control of your life as you will see that you play a significant role in making good things happen. You will also find that the more you do this exercise, the faster you get at coming up with three good things; you become aware and appreciative of many smaller things that you may not have noticed earlier.

• *The Lemonade:* I have been doing this exercise with my own children for many years. Today they still look forward to answering my "give me three things" request. Three good things will increase the chance of having some amazing dreams, which by itself will enhance your life satisfaction. The three good things exercise has been shown (by Dr. Martin Seligman) to increase happiness scores and decrease depression scores for up to six months (probably longer but that's as long as the study tested it). Turns out that study subjects were only supposed to participate for one week, but it was so easy and they felt so good afterward, that they continued doing "three good things" after the study was over.

74. 3 bad things

"Out of clutter find simplicity; from discord find harmony; in the middle of difficulty lies opportunity."
~Albert Einstein

"Turn your wounds into wisdom."   ~Oprah Winfrey

- *The Lemon:* Bad, bad, bad. That's the way it is! Imagining or remembering a multitude of "bad" things that happened to you during the day. Blaming and complaining without acknowledging or appreciating that you have some control.

- *Ingredients:* Acknowledgment – that "bad" things happen to you. Memory – what bad stuff occurred? Responsibility, Accountability, and Honesty – what was your role? Self-confidence and Self-worth – playing a role doesn't make you bad. Creativity – how could this actually be good? Respect, Kindness, Fairness, Empathy, Excuses and Forgiveness – try to release others from the blame. Blessings in disguise – if you don't look, you won't find them.

- *Preparation:* Acknowledge that there are things, people or events that make you frustrated, mad, angry, upset, depressed, or disappointed. Now just as with three good things, write down three bad things that happened during the day. These don't have to be horrible, devastatingly awful things; just anything that you would consider negative or "bad". Now focus on each item and try to ascertain what role you played in these situations. Did you instigate, motivate, or propagate? Assume and admit that you were somehow, at least in part, accountable. Assume the best about others who were involved. Show them respect and kindness; be fair in your assessment. Make excuses and empathize for them and finally, forgive them. Assume there are blessings in disguise. Now write about how this event or situation or thing was actually a good thing. You failed a test. There will be bigger tests and now you have a better idea about how to study for the rest of the year.

• *The Lemonade:* Daily conscious practice of turning apparent "bads" into "goods" is more than enlightening; it is empowering. You will feel more in control about your life and your destination. You will feel better about friends, family, coworkers, and even strangers. The process may seem difficult at first but will quickly become a fun project which will allow your creative lemonade to flow while you relieve your stress, depression, frustration, anger, and disappointment while enhancing your mental and emotional health, wellness, and happiness.

75. Develop and practice optimism

"Between the optimist and the pessimist, the difference is droll. The optimistic sees the doughnut; the pessimist the hole!" ~Oscar Wilde

"Optimism is essential to achievement and it is also the foundation of courage and true progress."
~Nicholas Murray Butler

• *The Lemon:* Pessimism. Fatalism. The glass is half-empty. My day sucked and this is representative of my life now and in the future.

• *Ingredients:* <u>Observe</u> – how you see yourself and your future. <u>Hope</u> – without hope, optimism is not possible.

• *Preparation:* Realize that you have a choice as to how you will view the world and your future. Optimism is partly genetically-determined; but there is a significant learned component which you can develop and practice. "I was born this way", doesn't provide a good excuse anymore. What can you do? Be aware of how you see yourself and how you interpret positive and negative events. If your initial reaction is, "oh no" or "damn it. Then you may be prone to a pessimistic self-explanatory style. Try to approach situations with a "how will this be good?" attitude. Learning optimism is adapted from Dr. Martin Seligman. Look at how you are assessing the incident. What is the belief that follows your assessment? Now what are the consequences of that belief? Do you feel better? Are you more motivated? Does this bring you closer to others? Improve your performance? If not, these are probably pessimistic thoughts. Dispute and argue with these thoughts; don't accept them. Take a step back to argue with your initial assessment. You are not stupid, slow, greedy, too short, etc. Provide sound arguments for these feelings. You can't argue with the beliefs and consequences because they are a logical outcome of your assessment. So change your assessment; you have the strength, knowledge, and power to do this. The results will be beliefs and consequences that will lead to positive self-improvement, enhanced self-assessment, and a brighter view for your future.

- *The Lemonade:* Optimists play a part in the positive outcomes that they experience. Optimists interpret their troubles as temporary and specific to a single situation and something under their control. Optimists are more likely to be married and to stay married. They get sick less often, complain less and have greater physical and emotional resilience. Optimists tend to be more successful at work, are more innovative and creative, and are more likely to feel a sense of engagement at work. Overall, they feel happier, have greater satisfaction with life, and live significantly longer than their pessimistic friends.

76. *Value process over product* (adapted from Dr. Ellen Langer)

"A process orientation not only sharpens our judgment, it makes us feel better about ourselves. A purely outcome orientation can take the joy out of life." ~Ellen Langer

• *The Lemon:* Being consumed by results and outcomes. Ignoring the process and the journey. Measuring success by whether you pass or fail will lead to emotional highs and lows, a perceived lack of control and a fear of defeat that can be paralyzing. Outcome orientation is a cause and symptom of being mindless.

• *Ingredients:* <u>Awareness</u> - of the steps along a pathway. <u>Patience</u> – what you learn on the journey is worth the wait. <u>Wisdom</u> – to know that just getting "the win" won't satisfy you. <u>Enthusiasm</u> – for what you may learn and discover. <u>Perseverance</u>, <u>Endurance</u>, <u>Fortitude</u> and <u>Resilience</u> – it may not be an easy journey. <u>Courage</u> – taking risks and pursuing your path.

• *Preparation:* If there is a pathway with no obstacles, it is often a dead-end. Don't judge performance by outcome. If you didn't care and you win a game, do you feel truly satisfied with the outcome? If you gave it everything you had and didn't win, you can still feel satisfied that you did what you could – no regrets. If you climb a mountain and don't look up until the summit, you'll miss a lot of beauty on the way. Consequently, if you never make the summit, you'll have wasted a lot of time for nothing. Thus, be aware of all the steps along the way; how you are feeling and what else is going on. Breaking something down into the individual steps allows you the freedom to make more conscious choices as the journey is continually reevaluated; decreased guilt and disappointment. When we think of inventors and discoverers, we tend to focus on the final product, invention, or discovery. We are impressed by their intellect and innovation and believe that we could never accomplish such a thing. When we learn about the detailed history of the invention or discovery, find out how many other people were involved, and what accidents contributed to the process, we are both less impressed and more likely to believe that even we could have possibly done the same thing in the same circumstances. Focusing on the process lets us see how other people and even luck may contribute to things or events that were previously foreboding; this helps us gain a sense of control and empowerment.

• *The Lemonade:* As Ellen Langer emphasizes, to be process-oriented is to be mindful. A process precedes every outcome; enjoy it. The process is where the learning, growing, and satisfaction take place. Being process-oriented hones our skills and our judgment. It allows us to focus on our attitudes, actions and responses; things we can control.

77. Donate your time

"Waste your time wisely." ~Sarena Farber

"If every American donated five hours a week, it would equal the labor of 20 million full-time volunteers."
~Whoopi Goldberg

• *The Lemon:* The belief that you have no time for anyone else. Time is better spent relaxing in front of the TV than volunteering to help others in need. Thinking that you are not wasting time.

• *Ingredients:* <u>Time</u> – we all have it. <u>Knowledge</u> – where your time will be well spent. <u>Generosity</u> and <u>Kindness</u> – treating people with goodwill. <u>Effort</u>, <u>Fairness</u> and <u>Attitude</u> – personal feelings of compassion and respect for others; not government-mandated "social justice" to keep everything equal. <u>Self-reliance</u> and <u>Cooperation</u> – donating time may pose many personal challenges and require a cooperative effort.

• *Preparation:* The pig and chicken are going to open a restaurant. The chicken wants to call it "Ham-N-Eggs". The pig responds, "For you it's only a contribution, for me it involves a lifetime commitment." We all have the time; but some of us don't spend it well. Donating time to those truly in need is one of the wisest choices we can make. Focus on others and empathize for their situation. What would you want others to do if it were you? This won't be easy. It may be one of the hardest things you've ever done. It may also be the most worthwhile, satisfying and fulfilling thing you've ever done. The choices are endless: build a house with Habitat for Humanity, be a Big Brother or Big Sister, teach inner city kids to read, lend a hand at an old-age home, or take a volunteer vacation with your family (Globalaware.org, projectsabroad.org, globalvolunteers.org, and many others). Contact a volunteer matching service such as volunteermatch.com, volunteersolutions.org or oyfp.org (On Your Feet Project) or hook up with one of a thousand organizations looking for volunteers. Use your skills and talents by donating your time to pass on knowledge – carpentry, plumbing, cash management, reading, mortgages, legal, medical, etc to people in need of these services.

• *The Lemonade:* Using your top strengths to help others is an effective and fulfilling means to improve your own long-term happiness and decrease depression; it raises our self-esteem, provides spiritual satisfaction, gives us a sense of helping the universe, and makes us a part of a broader community. You'll not only find time that you didn't know you had and feel phenomenal about how you're using it. Helping others helps us become more forgiving of our own inadequacies and limitations. Altruistic people tend to incur fewer stress-related illnesses and not surprisingly, live longer.

78. Achieve balance

"Just as your car runs more smoothly and requires less energy to go faster and farther when the wheels are in perfect alignment, you perform better when your thoughts, feelings, emotions, goals, and values are in balance."
~Brian Tracy

• *The Lemon:* Too much of a good thing is no longer a good thing. Without balance there is no harmony.

• *Ingredients:* <u>Time</u> – you've always got that. <u>Awareness</u> – of your needs. <u>Assessments</u> – where is your time is spent? <u>Wisdom</u> – where should your time really be spent? <u>Social intelligence</u> – what are the needs of those around you? <u>Moderation</u> – you can't do everything.

• *Preparation:* Balance does not mean equal time. Balance is subjective and implies a healthy equilibrium; where you feel the right amount of time and energy is spent. Everyone's needs are different. Where do you need to focus your time? Marriage, significant other, job, friends, children, finances, social life, exercise and physical health, spiritual life, community life, altruistic activities, and yourself. Physically, balance training is very important. It improves your performance, protects the body against injuries, and makes you more stable. Similarly, in balancing your life and your time, achieving balance will improve your overall mental and emotional performance, protect you from psychological ills, and allow you to be more secure and steady in all of your endeavors and relationships. Visualize your perfectly balanced day. List several things that you would like more of and less of to achieve your balance. Every day, decide what three things you will do to add the "more of" and/or reduce the "less of" list. Be realistic. Make sure that there is always some time devoted to you. Remember the balance between business, social and family life, the balance between physical activity and intellectual activity. What in your life do you feel deserves more attention? Have you been neglecting your spiritual life in exchange for extra time at work? You have the control to manipulate your time. Don't work on all of your weaknesses; focus on what is important to you for which you may have lost sight. Can you give too much in a relationship? Yes. If you are always just giving and not caring for yourself and the other person is just taking, this will lead to a dysfunctional, dependent, and unhealthy relationship in need of a balance check.

• *The Lemonade:* Achieving equilibrium in many aspects of your life. Creating balance in your life will reduce stress and enhance harmony and serenity. You will stop neglecting important areas and relationships in your life that deserve more attention and decrease ruminating about things that you already spend too much time on.

79. Develop and use emotional intelligence skills

"What really matters for success, character, happiness and life long achievement is a definite set of emotional skills – your EQ – not just purely cognitive abilities that are measured by IQ tests." ~ Daniel Goleman

• *The Lemon:* Not understanding, using or managing emotions or social skills. Being unaware of one's own emotional requirements. Being obtuse to others' needs and emotions.

• *Ingredients:* <u>Mindfulness</u> and <u>Situational awareness</u> – being fully present with attention to subtle and not so subtle cues and non-verbal forms of communication. <u>Interpersonal</u> and <u>intrapersonal skills</u> – social awareness and self-awareness. <u>Empathy</u> – a deep understanding and feeling for other people's point of view. <u>Curiosity</u> – trying to interpret the meaning of unspoken social signals. <u>Concern</u> – for the well-being of others.

• *Preparation:* You can't truly love or relate well to others if you don't love and relate well to yourself. Whether emotional and social intelligence are truly separate kinds of intelligences or skill sets that represent cognitive intelligence is unclear. What is clear is that you will benefit in many ways from knowing how you function and what makes you click. Being able to perceive, understand, use and manage your emotions is a very useful and functional talent that requires innate ability and an understanding of a situation as well as the players involved. It is impossible to understand the inner workings of others until you at least start to get a grasp of your own social and emotional life. Looking for and understanding subtle non-verbal forms of communication and being mindful of what others may be trying to indicate, will greatly enhance all of your personal and professional relationships. This is more than just perceiving and expressing emotions; it is understanding and consciously managing emotions.

- *The Lemonade:* Having a great grasp of your social skills and emotions and being able to relate on this level to others. Mastering emotional and social skills will help improve your resilience and your ability to relate to friends, families, coworkers, and strangers. Having honed social and emotional skills yields benefits in academic achievement, performance issues, and significantly more positive behavior. In the working world, those with higher emotional intelligence are more likely to be seen at mid career as having high leadership potential. It will help you solve everyday problems and even help you make moral decisions. Don't leave home without this emotional lemonade.

80. Let go of the past

"Finish each day and be done with it. You have done what you could; some blunders and absurdities have crept in; forget them as soon as you can. Tomorrow is a new day; you shall begin it serenely and with too high a spirit to be encumbered with your old nonsense."
~ Ralph Waldo Emerson

"Yesterday is history. Tomorrow is a mystery. And today? Today is a gift. That's why they call it the present."
~ Babatunde Olatunji

• *The Lemon:* Living in the past and having the present stolen from you. Comparing what was instead of focusing on what is.

• *Ingredients:* Mindfulness and Continual Awareness – focus on the present. Forgiveness – of yourself and others. Enthusiasm – excitement for what's going on around you. Determination – to not allow yourself to be drawn into the temptations of the past. Strength and Self-confidence – being self-assured to deal with the now.

• *Preparation:* Letting go of the past can be one of the hardest things to do. The first step is to be aware of thoughts of the past or ruminating memories. Respect these memories. Ignoring or denying them won't help them go away. Letting go of the past means understanding that you can't relive it or change it. You can look at it, admit it, accept it, and move on mentally. You did the best you could at the time – now it's done. Maybe you would make a different decision today; that's a great thing.

You've shown that you have changed and grown. You may benefit from a brief analysis and evaluation of why and how you made a decision, but don't ruminate on this. More time focusing on the past takes time away from being able to make the correct decisions now. Forgive yourself and find forgiveness for others. This puts you in control and removes your role as a victim. Let go of the disappointments and the anger. Even letting go of the "good" times will help you feel better about today. Traditional psychotherapy focused on the past – how has it affected you today? Positive psychological counseling concentrates on more present-minded techniques such as self-efficacy (belief that you can succeed in certain situations), forgiveness, and the use of strengths.

• *The Lemonade:* This is the greatest time in your life. Right now. This doesn't mean that you shouldn't have fond memories of the past and brief reminiscences when looking at memorabilia and old photo albums. You are the only one who can control your letting go of the past. It is empowering to put the past in perspective and realize that it does not control your future. Today determines your future. Move beyond the self-destructive behavior that memories and unresolved anger bring and be liberated by removing the shackles of the past.

Neil E. Farber, M.D., PhD.

81. Exercise-induced wellness

"The only exercise some people get is jumping to conclusions, running down their friends, side-stepping responsibility, and pushing their luck!"
~Author Unknown

"Physical activity is an excellent stress-buster and provides other health benefits as well. It also can improve your mood and self image." ~Jon Wickham

• *The Lemon:* Inactivity, laziness, poor physical health, disease, and fatigue.

• *Ingredients:* <u>Drive</u>, <u>Motivation</u> and <u>Goals</u> – to look/feel better, lose weight, become healthier, meet new people, etc. If your goal is simply to exercise, this doesn't typically last long. <u>Mindfulness</u> – what are you achieving? <u>Creativity</u> – something new. <u>Shoes</u> – unless you're swimming. <u>Bravery</u> – go beyond your typical limits. <u>Time</u> – it doesn't have to take much. <u>Friends</u> – if you don't have them, you will after exercising. <u>Enthusiasm</u> – find something you like to do.

• *Preparation:* Get off the couch! 20-30 minutes of exercise stimulates feelings of well-being, increases energy and releases tension. Join a gym, participate in a Pilates or yoga class, or connect with a running group or tennis club. Walk around the block, dust off your old bike or jump in a pool, lake or ocean for a swim. Don't worry about how fast you are. Set goals of doing something that you enjoy, so that you stay motivated to accomplish this. Walk on a treadmill while reading a good book, listening to your favorite music, or watching TV. Don't start with activities that you won't enjoy doing for a long time. Make this exercise fun and fulfilling. Take the dance class that you've been putting off. Learn a new skill that you've always been interested in – golf, tennis, racquet ball, skating, rowing, etc. No excuses or blaming someone or something for not participating – just do it!

• *The Lemonade:* A healthy mind in a healthy body. Regular exercise helps strengthen our mind-body connections. These aren't just new age fads; there are scientifically proven links between your psychological self and your physical self. Exercise lowers blood pressure, increases muscle strength and flexibility, maintains strong bones, improves heart and lung capacities, and enhances immune function – to keep you healthier and living longer. Healthy physical activities play an important role in creating a positive mindset, in part because exercise releases feel-good endorphins and reduces stress, anxiety, and depression while helping us feel more relaxed and happy. Exercise also helps us on a positive path by providing social interactions with like-minded people who care about their bodies and boosting our self-confidence levels to new highs.

82. *You are what you eat*

"Eating is not merely a material pleasure. Eating well gives a spectacular joy to life and contributes immensely to goodwill and happy companionship. It is of great importance to the morale." ～Elsa Schiaparelli

"Happiness is.....finding two olives in your martini when you're hungry." ～ Johnny Carson

• *The Lemon:* Not caring what goes on in your body. Fear filled eating. Depression and negativity can lead to increased, unhealthy eating. Drowning your sorrows in an ice-cream Sunday...

• *Ingredients:* <u>Portion regulate</u> – eat when hungry, stop when satisfied. <u>Mindfulness</u> – maximum flavor per mouthful. <u>Curiosity</u> and <u>Courage</u> – trying new foods opens your mind and your palate. <u>Moderation</u> – resist reckless temptations. <u>Creativity</u> – recipe possibilities are endless. <u>Relaxation</u> – don't eat when stressed.

• *Preparation:* Don't eat in secret. Don't deprive yourself. Don't binge. Eat mindfully. Don't just eat - savor every bite; slow down. Appreciate the sensations of smelling, tasting, chewing, and swallowing. Eat with gratitude for whoever made, served, processed, and sold the food; include God or the universe for giving us the gifts with which to process. Food should be a pleasure not something feared. Appreciate that food is something that you need for energy and health. Respecting your body means that you should want to provide the best fuel to make it run most efficiently and last a long time. Relax when you eat. Under stress the digestive system doesn't function optimally and people eat more unhealthy sweets and snacks. Eat foods you love, even ice cream in moderation. Eat Omega 3 foods, like pumpkin or hemp seeds, fish, spinach, or walnuts to help you fight binges, depression, and weight gains. Find joy in soy. Stock your freezer with healthier frozen snacks. Use sugar free, calorie free, fat free or "light" substitutes. Replace salt with other spices that you like. Try healthy spreads instead of margarine or butter. Have at least one night a week designated as vegetarian night – be inventive. Try different whole wheat products until you find one that you like. Look at ingredients before you buy.

• *The Lemonade:* Eating happy and healthy foods. Being able to find joy and satisfaction in eating without fear. Eating foods that you like and feeling great about it. I'm not promoting fad diets or any diets. I'm suggesting a lifestyle change that encourages joyful, healthy eating which will become a habit and last a lifetime. Sitting down to eat a relaxing, healthy, scrumptious meal with friends and family.

83. Replace "have to" with "want to"

"I believe that by changing my point of view about anything I can turn it from a Have-to into a Want-to. The trick is in knowing my life purpose and in taking a position that makes this activity on-purpose for me rather than counter-purpose. (If the activity is truly counter to my life purpose, I shouldn't be doing it.)"

~ Richard Brodie

- *The Lemon:* The belief that you have no control of your life and your destiny. There is always someone or something else to blame who is making you do things; e.g. "You *have to* eat this lemon."

- *Ingredients:* Self-confidence and Courage – to make the right choices and pursue them. Responsibility and Accountability – for your thoughts, feelings and actions. Goals, Purpose and Meaning – help guide your path. Perseverance – fortitude in not giving up in the face of challenges. CHOICE – it's all yours.

- *Preparation:* No, you don't "have to". Whether it is something fun like going to a movie with your kids, dinner on a blind date, or vacation with the in-laws, you have choices. Even things that you probably consider necessary like paying bills, working, and eating are still optional. We think of each of them as a "have to" because the consequences of not doing them may be undesirable. That means that you have analyzed and assessed the situation and have chosen the best option based on your future goals and plans; you've just made a "have to" to "want to" conversion. Adapting a "want to" attitude involves goal-setting and having a purpose-driven life. So, set some short-term and long-term goals. Many "want to's" get misinterpreted as "have to's" because it seems like there's no alternative such as having a job and paying your mortgage. Appreciate that there are many people who don't do either. These are options. If your goal is to be able to provide food, shelter, and clothing for your family, then you will probably want to pay your mortgage and to do that, you may want to hold onto that job.

- *The Lemonade:* You are mad at your boss. You blame him and complain to everyone who will listen that you wish you didn't have to go to work for him. Guess what? You don't! No one is making you – but you. If you go through all the reasons why you are working and decide that it is better to continue working there, then you have made that choice. Now view this as a "want to" not a "have to" and appreciate that going to work at this job is a choice. Your happiness and satisfaction with life will increase and stress, frustration, and depression will decrease when you truly believe that you have choices and verbalize a "want to" rather than a "have to".

Making Lemonade

DESSERTS

84. Have integrity

"If you have integrity, nothing else matters. If you don't have integrity, nothing else matters." ~Alan Simpson

- *The Lemon:* Being incomplete, dishonest.

- *Ingredients:* Respect – having reverence or value for others. Confidence – in yourself and others. Empathy – the world through someone else's eyes. Loyalty – making lasting commitments. Genuineness – authentic and open. Fairness – respect for justice. Modesty – realizing that you can't know it all. Conscientiousness – thoroughness in accomplishing tasks. Sincerity and Honesty – virtuous truthfulness. Belief in something greater – universal guiding and ethical principles.

- *Preparation:* Have a belief system that is unfaltering and unwavering in the face of adversity. Develop and maintain your own code of ethics and be consistent with these values and principles in your thoughts, feelings, attitudes, and actions. Your code should be built on a strong foundation of respect, fairness, loyalty, and empathy for others. Stand strong against outside influences that try to sway you from your values. Keep your word when you give it. Do the right thing because you know it is the right thing to do, not because someone else might be looking.

- *The Lemonade:* Having consistent actions, values, and principles. Being and feeling complete mentally and psychosocially. Being reliable and honorable; with sound moral principles. Living according to your convictions will create a strong sense of harmony and serenity. Making decisions based on these moral and ethical convictions and values will lead you to become a friend, confidant, coworker, and significant other who can be trusted and relied on for advice or a shoulder to lean on. It will also fill you with integrity energy (better than the 5-hour stuff).

85. *Seek to achieve flow* (adapted from Dr. Mihaly Csikszentmihalyi)

"The flow experience, like everything else, is not "good" in an absolute sense. It is good only in that it has the potential to make life more rich, intense, and meaningful; it is good because it increases the strength and complexity of the self." ~Mihaly Csikszentmihalyi

• *The Lemon:* Time spent being anxious or bored. Performing meaningless activities. Not being fully involved. Watching the clock slow down as you do a job or perform some boring activity.

• *Ingredients:* Self-aware – of your needs, strengths, abilities, interests. Goals – helps recognize challenges and make choices. Mindfulness and Immersion – put everything into what you're doing. Genuineness – being open, honest and receptive to new experiences. Passion, Joy, and Courage – can't hold back. Self-assurance with humility – confidence in yourself and something greater.

• *Preparation:* We're talking about optimal experiences. Feeling in control of your actions. Doing an activity that is somewhat difficult but you have the abilities and skills to perform it. You are "in the zone" and hours fly by in seconds. One sure way to avoid happiness is to spend time trying to find it. Rather, happiness comes from being involved in activities that we enjoy and there are no activities that we enjoy more than those in which we find flow. Seek to achieve flow by finding activities, hobbies, and jobs which utilize your strengths, skills, talents and interests; happiness will be the best side effect that you've ever experienced. You cannot achieve flow passively, you have to go out there and make it happen. Flow can happen during music, building, reading, writing, philosophy, biking, skiing, basketball, karate, dancing, singing, bird watching, golf, tennis, hiking, knitting, sewing, cooking, baking, eating, gardening, hockey, computer games, math, yoga, Pilates, archery, gymnastics, surgery, listening to music, vacuuming, cleaning, filling out taxes, painting, chess, praying, running, poetry, etc, etc.

• *The Lemonade:* Being in flow is not always a pleasurable, joyful experience; sometimes it's even uncomfortable or painful – but you don't care because it is so satisfying. Finding flow is empowering and exhilarating. Implicit in flow-related activities is that you don't need any external motivation or reward; just being involved in the activity is motivating and rewarding for its own sake. Finding flow will help you find happiness and positivity in life. You will also find a sense of fulfillment as you demonstrate (to yourself) that you can overcome challenges and use your talents and abilities to achieve and accomplish. You are in control.

86. Use your signature strengths in new ways
(adapted from Dr. Martin Seligman)

"Herein is my formulation of the good life: Using your signature strengths every day in the main realms of your life to bring abundant gratification and authentic happiness."
~Martin Seligman

• *The Lemon:* Same old lemon. Day in and day out. Being bored, uninterested and disengaged.

• *Ingredients:* Self-awareness – to understand you. Creativity – inventive and innovative. Curiosity – to really investigate who you are. Self-worth, Dedication, and Fortitude – to perform at your peak.

• *Preparation:* Almost everyone can identify positive characteristic strengths that define and excite them. Assess your strengths (there are more than twenty in all) and identify your top five (signature) strengths. Pick one of your signature strengths and use it in a new way every day for one week. Find new creative and innovative applications for your signature strengths. Some examples: strength = vitality: 1) do the same old thing with more vigor and energy, 2) engage in a rigorous physical activity, 3) attend a performance of something, 4) watch a comedy show or movie, 5) do any kind of outdoor activity, 6) call an old roommate, 7) take a yoga class, 8) stargaze at night, 9) write thank you or appreciation notes to the people at work who make a difference. There is no limit to the number of choices you have. For an added bonus, try to use some of these strengths at work.

Make a detailed list of activities that you are required or asked to do at your work. Now try to visualize how you could apply your signature strengths to these actions. When you are doing the same job with a better attitude, your results will be better.

- *The Lemonade:* Exercising your strengths is fulfilling. Using your strengths in new ways will decrease depression and lead you along a path of happiness. I'm not just talking happy for a few days. Using signature strengths in new ways has been shown to lead to long-term happiness. Life will become more exciting as you are able to apply techniques, skills, and talents in which you are already great, to a unique activity or event. When you do this at work, even doing the same job that you have been doing every day, will result in better performance, better outcome, more happiness, and greater satisfaction.

87. Practice acts of loving-kindness

"Too often we underestimate the power of a touch, a smile, a kind word, a listening ear, an honest compliment, or the smallest act of caring, all of which have the potential to turn a life around." ~Leo Buscaglia

• *The Lemon:* Spending time thinking about oneself. Self-centeredness. Being engrossed in your computer, television or cell phone. Performing mindless activities for no apparent reason.

• *Ingredients:* Generosity – true sense of giving. Love – heartfelt. Kindness – toward friend and foe. Empathy – what do others' really want? Altruism and Philanthropy – a selfless concern for the welfare of others. Gratitude and Forgiveness – amazing gifts for you and all of the recipients.

• *Preparation:* Break out of the daily grind and spend time showing others how you care. Make quality time for yourself. Start with small acts of purposeful and deliberate kindness, so that they are for the intended recipient. Begin with yourself. Buy yourself a gift, forgive yourself for something you've done, recognize one of your strengths or talents, etc. Next try those who you feel especially fond of, like family and close friends, or perhaps people in high regard like clergy or spiritual leaders. Then you might try acts of lovingkindness with coworkers and other acquaintances. Now try to perform these acts for total strangers and finally, move on to people with whom you've have strained or downright hostile relationships. The least you can give to someone; your time, a brief (but sincere smile), or a friendly hello. These will be (with practice) easy to give, but will be more meaningful than you would ever believe for the recipient.

- *The Lemonade:* Acts of loving-kindness cost nothing to perform and the benefits are out of this world. Acts of kindness, love and generosity form the backbone of productive societies. Not government sanctioned charity but giving from the heart. We get inspired and invigorated if we are lucky enough to see, experience or be the recipients of others performing acts of kindness. When we perform acts of kindness, we benefit from the giving. It softens and opens our hearts and opens the universe to deliver more blessings and let the sun shine down upon us. Kindness helps people feel respected and broadens our perspective. Kindness makes kindness; it's a pay-it-forward system.

88. *The power of possibility*

"Limitations live only in our minds. But if we use our imaginations, our possibilities become limitless."

~Jamie Paolinetti

• *The Lemon:* Thinking in terms of limitations, rather than possibilities. Status quo. "We know how this will turn out…"

• *Ingredients:* Creativity – the limits are only what we make them. Open Mindedness – the future is a blank slate. Curiosity – what could it be? Box – now think outside of it. Perspectives – maintain multiple. Questions – ask many. Answers – less important than the questions. Perseverance – a commitment to the belief in the power of possibility. Enthusiasm - embracing and anticipating the journey. Hope – the best is going to happen.

• *Preparation:* Adapted from Ellen Langer's *Counterclockwise* book – Start by assuming that you don't know what you can do or become. This allows you to remove your side blinders and look around at the enormous possibilities of what you could be. The illusion of stability and that is the way it is, not only prevents us from exploring alternatives; we don't even think of asking the questions that could start the journey. When you learn something new, maintain a little healthy doubt. Look at things from a different angle, a new perspective. Don't categorize information into a stereotype; ask fresh questions. It is nearly impossible to prove something is impossible; but easy to prove it is possible by doing it. Our minds are the doorways to limitation and stagnation or possibility and opportunity. You have the choice of walking along a well-groomed path on which you've traveled to the destination that you've been or forging your own unchartered course to a destination that you've only dreamt about. It can all start with two important words: What if?

• *The Lemonade:* Exploring possibilities is empowering. It is like interviewing yourself for a new job position that you want to create or being in the witness protection program and starting your life again. Go anywhere - do anything. It can't get more exciting than this! There is much to learn and that much of what we know and are sure of, may turn out to be incorrect in the future. Even science and medical texts may change the facts in the next edition. I know because I've written them! Open your mind to unending and limitless alternatives rather than what "is" and what "should be".

89. Help create your personal job description

"Just as energy is the basis of life itself, and ideas the source of innovation, so is innovation the vital spark of all human change, improvement and progress". ~Ted Levitt

- *The Lemon:* Job burnout. Dissatisfaction at work. Not being engaged or being actively disengaged at work where you're usually just a paycheck away from quitting.

- *Ingredients:* <u>Self-awareness</u> – know yourself and your strengths. <u>Flexibility</u> and <u>Open-mindedness</u> – be open to the possibilities. <u>Curiosity</u> – look for and visualize the possibilities. <u>Creativity</u> – what can you do with what you have?

- *Preparation:* Identify opportunities to make your job more you; more fulfilling. Try to look at your job as if you were a consultant, hired to make the job more effective or more efficient; more streamlined. What would you recommend? Your job is not set in stone and mortar, it is movable blocks which you have the flexibility of organizing in a way that will enhance your satisfaction and performance. Visualize how the job may be redesigned to increase the organization and proficiency while making better use of your talents, skills, and strengths. This is the most important factor. You need to feel intrinsically motivated by having the job involve strengths that you want to use.

- *The Lemonade:* Job crafting; turning the job that you have into the job that you want. Employees making changes to their own designs that bring about positive outcomes such as engagement, satisfaction, resilience, and thriving. This won't just change the job and help you, this will help the business and organization, because when you are engaged enough and care enough about your work to change the job to be more in line with your strengths, the job will also benefit. Being able to use your strengths at your job will allow you to work in flow and with passion. This is a great way to transition from working a job to being fully engaged and dedicated in what you feel you should be doing with your life.

90. Concentrate on creativity

"It is better to create than to be learned, creating is the true essence of life." ~Barthold Georg Niebuhr

"The principle goal of education is to create men who are capable of doing new things, not simply of repeating what other generations have done - men who are creative, inventive and discoverers." ~Jean Piaget

- *The Lemon:* Unimaginative. Lack of common sense. Looking at the clouds for shapes and just seeing clouds. Thinking "there's nothing to do around here today."

- *Ingredients:* Inventiveness – having the ingenuity. Imagination – never leave home without it. Vision – more than what you can see. Inspiration and Motivation – from within. Resourceful – appreciating what there is to work with. Originality – that no one has done it before is a positive not a negative. Development – seeing potential. Enthusiasm – for what you'll create. Courage – to go beyond the typical.

- *Preparation:* Imagine. Brainstorm. Visualize. Problem-solve. Follow hunches. Follow intuition. Be an innovator. Try to find a different path, develop a brand new trail, or facilitate networking to bring new people together. Wear clothing that you wouldn't normally wear. Think out of the box. Look at things through appreciative eyes. View the world through the eyes of a child where everything old is new again. As Abraham Maslow indicated, if all you have in your toolbox is a hammer, then everything looks like a nail. Don't just allow yourself to make mistakes, but take advantages of the mistakes and use them in an innovative and inventive way. Have confidence; people are much less creative when they are intimidated or being judged (including self-criticism). Creativity flourishes in environments that are reinforcing and supportive. Creativity is at a high when we are in middle-focus; free from obligatory reasoning (high focus) and emotional overtones (low focus).

• *The Lemonade:* Boosting your creative juices is within your capabilities. Everyone can do it. The ability to apply inventiveness and imagination; innovation is a characteristic of leaders. Losing your fear of being wrong is exhilarating. Generating novel ideas and solutions to overcome obstacles or make things work better or more efficiently is empowering. Here's a positive cycle: well-being enhances creativity and creativity, in turn, leads to well-being and happiness.

91.   Be persistent

"Nothing in this world can take the place of persistence. Talent will not; nothing is more common than unsuccessful people with talent. Genius will not; unrewarded genius is almost a proverb. Education will not; the world is full of educated derelicts. Persistence and determination alone are omnipotent. The slogan "press on" has solved and always will solve the problems of the human race."   ~Calvin Coolidge

• *The Lemon:* Giving up without a fight. Feeble attempts at making things work. Accepting a "no" answer when something is important to you.

• *Ingredients:* Perseverance – commitment to your goal. Determination, Motivation and Resilience – to pursue a noble path despite challenges. Consistency – constant, reliable and stable. Passion – zest, vigor, excitement and enthusiasm.

• *Preparation:* Maintain forward, positive actions, regardless of your feelings. You may have brief flashes of a desire to quit; but don't give in to these. You are able to find motivation from inside your heart and soul because you know what you are doing is right and worth pursuing. Realize that thoughts and intentions won't produce the goals. Only your actions produce visible results. Appreciate the difference between persistence and stubbornness. If you're no longer still inspired, no longer see a purpose or have changed your thinking, then reconsidering your goal and altering your plans may be the wisest course of action.

Persistence is made easier when it is in the context of following your dream or what you believe to be your destiny or what you know is right or what you have as a vision. If you feel strongly about something; use this as your intrinsic motivation and your little internal whip to keep your butt moving in the proper direction.

- *The Lemonade:* Having perseverance. Being determined to fulfill, accomplish and achieve something that is important to you. Being persistent allows you to continue to pursue your goal regardless of extrinsic motivation, challenges, or apparent obstacles. Another positive cycle: the more persistent you are, the more you'll achieve, accomplish, and appreciate that persistence paid off. Both the results and the process will be self-motivating and encourage you to persist. For example: you are adherent to an exercise schedule, you lose weight, you look better, your clothes fit better, you've got more energy, and are more encouraged to continue the exercise schedule. Unstoppable lemonade.

Neil E. Farber, M.D., PhD.

92. Become wise

"Wisdom is the right use of knowledge. To know is not to be wise. Many men know a great deal, and are all the greater fools for it. There is no fool so great a fool as a knowing fool. But to know how to use knowledge is to have wisdom."
~Charles Spurgeon

• *The Lemon:* Believing that what you know is true and complete. Not learning from experience. Inflexibility. Not learning how to cope with challenges. Not finding balance in your life.

• *Ingredients:* <u>Humility</u> – not self-absorbed. <u>Objectivity</u> and <u>Mindfulness</u> – view situations nonjudgmentally. <u>Knowledge</u> – logic, book smart. <u>Understanding</u> – emotional intelligence. <u>Flexibility</u> – open to new information. <u>Curiosity</u> – search for new information. <u>Adaptability</u> – resilient and coping. <u>Empathy</u> - "other centered".

• *Preparation:* Admit that you don't know much (neither do I). Observe with an open mind; not just around you, but also inside of you. You can help this process; throw away your ego for a little while. Don't let it get in the way of making the right choices. The more you experience, the more opportunities you have to learn. There's the old adage that wisdom comes with age, but sometimes age just comes alone. It doesn't just happen. You have to invite it in. Take an active role. Don't just experience; learn from experience. Knowledge is power. You have the opportunity to use everything that you've ever learned. There is no wasted knowledge. All of the advice in the Biblical book of Proverbs centers around the word, "wisdom". This was the path to success and blessings in life. Wisdom is distinct from being smart. Wisdom also involves having life management skills. The word for wisdom in Hebrew is chochmah, which is also called the life-force of all creation. This is not a coincidence. Chochmah, as in wisdom, is a balanced combination of heart and mind. Act after deliberation rather than react. Being flexible and comfortable knowing that most of our factual knowledge is not absolute, is a great first step toward wisdom. Your mental skills are malleable. Wisdom can be divided into *cognitive* (acquiring), *reflective* (analyzing) and affective (emotional) components. Brain areas associated with the affective component of wisdom do increase activity with age.

• *The Lemonade:*   Through enhanced personal safety, security, and well-being, wisdom builds confidence without self-absorption. Wisdom helps us see impermanence in the world which improves our flexibility, resiliency, and adaptability to change. Wisdom is associated with happiness and life satisfaction. In fact, wisdom has a stronger, positive effect on life satisfaction than does objective life circumstances. You'd be wise to make this lemonade.

93. Practice positive parenting

"Parents are often so busy with the physical rearing of children that they miss the glory of parenthood, just as the grandeur of the tree is lost when raking leaves."
~Marcelene Cox

"Life affords no greater responsibility, no greater privilege, than the raising of the next generation."
~Dr. C. Everett Koop

The Lemon: Arguing, scolding and feeling lousy about your parenting skills. Not having the knowledge or will to promote responsibility and positive attitudes in your children.

•   *Ingredients:* <u>Love</u> – that's a guarantee. <u>Trust</u> – in yourself and your children's abilities. <u>Fairness</u> – treat all the kids equally. <u>Perseverance</u> – it's not always easy. <u>Forgiveness</u> – when you are disappointed. <u>Responsibility</u> – this is *your* job. <u>Hope</u> – remain optimistic about the outcome. <u>Knowledge</u> – how to become and remain a positive model for your children. <u>Humor</u> – it helps.

•   *Preparation:* While there are many other factors involved, authoritative parenting is most likely to produce responsible, curious, and outgoing children; positive attitudes, and behaviors. Encourage responsibility & initiative, develop good decision-making skills, encourage resistance to peer pressure, and promote cooperation and successful attitudes. Encourage and nurture optimism; develop optimistic self-explanatory thinking. Support strong family ties and values. Encourage children to achieve and do things they've never done before; developing flow and strengths. Help them move beyond their fears to see problems as challenges. Use consequences (directly linked to a specific behavior, proactive and proportionate), rather than punishments (irrespective of the offensive act, reactive, and excessive). Praise when there is something praiseworthy. Don't falsely raise self-esteem which may later lead to passivity and depression. Put a stop to toxic, mindless complaining, and blaming. Provide unconditional love, warmth, and affection. Teach them gratitude and forgiveness. Encourage courage, curiosity, creativity, conscientiousness, and humor. Teach and encourage mindfulness. Be the example, be the example and be the example.

• *The Lemonade:* Fostering positive emotions in your children. Raising optimistic, responsible, happy children with high self-efficacy who are socially comfortable. Kids modeling your positive and optimistic attitudes and behaviors while developing their own signature strengths, goals, and purposes. Witnessing our children growing and developing like this not only makes us proud parents, but it gives our lives more purpose and meaning.

94. Don't take anyone for granted

"If human beings are perceived as potentials rather than problems, as possessing strengths instead of weaknesses, as unlimited rather than dull and unresponsive, then they thrive and grow to their capabilities." ～Barbara Bush

"You can easily judge the character of a man by how he treats those who can do nothing for him."
～James D. Miles

• *The Lemon:* Expecting someone or something to always be available; to serve you without recognition or gratitude. Failing to appreciate a good deed, helpful hand, or just someone's company.

• *Ingredients:* Empathy and Social Intelligence – what would they want? What would you want? Respect – feelings and actions. Gratitude – truly appreciating the effort of others. Forgiveness – let go of predisposing negative feelings. Altruism – do this for others.

• *Preparation:* Be free with your praise, affection, adoration, gratitude, and appreciation. Try to be empathetic to the motivation, effort, and time that someone used to help you. Believe that the other person had many other jobs, duties, and responsibilities with which to attend (because I know they did). Believe that they had a choice (because they truly did) about whether or not to be there for you. Conclude that they were present or helped not because they were supposed to, but because they wanted to. Do not assume that you know what they are thinking. Do not assume that because they do not have a big smile in place, that they are not satisfied with their ability to help you. Perhaps something devastating, demoralizing, or depressing recently occurred in their lives, how would this have affected you? Perhaps adding praise and gratitude would bring positive change to their day. This is much healthier for them and for you than criticizing, complaining, or ignoring.

• *The Lemonade:* Truly appreciating others. It not only doesn't cost you anything but the rewards for giving these valuable gifts are enormous. The gifts of giving selflessly and altruism are plentiful. When you focus on appreciating others and not taking them for granted, you put the needs of others ahead of your own. You will be blessed with expanding social circles and healthier relationships. You will become a trusted and reliable friend and a coworker with whom people will want to interact. You'll also reap other health and wellness benefits such as an enhanced immune system, a "helper's high", stress reduction, improved mood, confidence, and self-esteem, and an overall better satisfaction with life. Don't take this lemonade for granted.

95. *Practice problem solving*

"Don't dwell on what went wrong. Instead, focus on what to do next. Spend your energies on moving forward toward finding the answer." ~Denis Waitley

"It's not that I'm so smart, it's just that I stay with problems longer." ~Albert Einstein

- *The Lemon:* Worrying about problems and feeling sorry for yourself. Looking for the "Win" when you're in an argument or trying to avoid discussions.

- *Ingredients:* Relaxation – start with a deep breath and a calm attitude. Social & Emotional intelligence – understanding your emotions and those of others. Insight and Perspective – you have the power to change how you view problems. Empathy – helps you look for the win-win. Respect – fair play in conflicts. Appreciative inquiry – what is right, not what is wrong. Abstraction, Creativity, and Lateral Thinking – out of the box solutions. Brainstorming – you're not on your own.

- *Preparation:* How you think about problems is actually helping to solve the problem. RELAX. Big deep breath. Viewing "problems" as challenges, situations, or even as obstacles, allows you to look at them with more vigor and enthusiasm. Don't look at them as a burden; believe that there is a valid reason for this to be happening and that the answer will be a win-win situation that will be mutually beneficial for you and any other party. Use appreciative inquiry to find out what was best about the situation in the past, think about what worked well then, envision what you would want in the future that would involve using your strengths. Visualize some potential solutions and then discuss some options while getting feedback from any other interested person. Try to envision several direct and indirect consequences of these proposals. How are you affected? How about others? Put yourself in their position. Would you be happy with this outcome? How does this proposal affect other systems and other people? In addition to the cognitive skills of figuring out logistics, problem solving requires proper motivation, attitude, positive emotions, and realistic optimism.

• *The Lemonade:* With proper problem solving skills and abilities, correct action can be taken to alleviate potentially detrimental situations or failures. By being open-minded to possibilities, one may be able to eliminate potential product or process failures. When you are able to arrive at a win-win solution, you feel better, more satisfied, and more fulfilled. Your faith and trust in others is enhanced as is your faith and trust in some greater purpose for your life.

96. *Choose optimalism over perfectionism*
(adapted from Dr. Tal Ben-Shahar)

"In essence, Perfectionists reject everything that deviates from their flawless, faultless ideal vision, and as a result they suffer whenever they do not meet their own unrealistic standards. Optimalists accept, and make the best of, everything that life has to offer."

~Tal Ben-Shahar

• *The Lemon:* Viewing life as a straight line; being afraid of failure; being rigid and critical; setting unrealistic goals and focusing on the outcome rather than the journey.

• *Ingredients:* Active acceptance and Mindfulness – being aware of how things, not what you're hoping they'll be and adjusting your emotions and course of action accordingly. Coping and Resilience – feedback is learning is growth. Flexibility and Adaptability – look forward to changes and be willing to adjust your path. Failure, Emotions, Success and Reality – accept them and savor them.

• *Preparation:* To become an optimalist, accept reality and set high, but attainable goals and standards. Focus on both the outcome and the journey with a genuine curiosity and desire to learn. Learn from failure. Value flexibility, adaptability, and the experiences (both positive and negative) that come with changes in your life. Perfectionists want to look good and they view feedback as criticism. Instead, value the process and the experiences that you will take away. Take risks and actually seek out feedback for self-improvement and learning. Appreciate and savor success but don't be afraid of failure. Learn to find satisfaction in a less-than-perfect environment and after a less-than-perfect performance. Give yourself permission to be human and fallible. Make decisions as a satisficer rather than a maximizer. A satisficer looks for high quality yet when their criteria are met, can accept the "good enough". Maximizers, on the other hand, to get the best of whatever it is they are looking for, spend a lot of time, energy, and anxiety during decision making to get "the perfect."

• *The Lemonade:* Maximizers may be more financially successful, but satisfiers have less regrets, blame themselves less, and are more satisfied with life, Being an optimalist is an adaptive and healthy form of positive perfectionism. The optimalists "good enough" mindset yields greater energy, improved resilience, and better coping and learning. These benefits, in turn, result in more self-confidence, self-acceptance, self-esteem, and greater intrinsic motivation to take on new challenges. In total, optimalists will experience a richer, more emotional life.

97. Help a friend

"A true friend knows your weaknesses but shows you your strengths; feels your fears but fortifies your faith; sees your anxieties but frees your spirit; recognizes your disabilities but emphasizes your possibilities."
⁓William Arthur Ward

• *The Lemon:* Saying, "If there's anything you need just let me know" immediately before you hang up the phone.

• *Ingredients:* A friend – can't help one without having one. Empathy, Compassion, Social Intelligence, and Communication – this is all about someone else and how you relate to them. Flexibility – you may have to bend physically and mentally. Listen – often more important than speaking.

• *Preparation:* During a time of great need, even a close friend may not be able to ask for help. What can you do? It depends on the friend's needs. Ask them what they would like help with and listen not only to their words but to their nonverbal clues. Don't be limited to what you would want if you were them. They may have other concerns or priorities. Some suggestions. For friends who are sick: offer words of encouragement, suggestions for improving their health, drop off some food, movies, or books, help cook a meal, do laundry, clean the house, pick up kids or run errands. For the friend who is isolated (no family in town): take them out for meals, introduce them to committees, clubs, organizations or religious institutions in which to become involved, take them to the library, local bookstores, or fun shops, have them join you in a class (yoga, Pilates, knitting, etc), help them find a place that specializes in one of their hobbies. For all friends in general be patient, reliable, consistent, available, gentle, and comforting. Try not to offer advice in hindsight like, "That wasn't the smartest thing to do." Most of us realize that hindsight is much better than foresight. Everyone grieves at his or her own pace. Listen. Help them find humor without making light of their situation. Don't be an enabler; covering up for them for missed obligations, or someone who supports excuses that you think will cause them harm.

• *The Lemonade:* Helping friends opens our hearts and souls. It reinforces one of our important purposes in this world to support each other. Helping friends is not just good for the friends but also for us. Every time we give without expecting anything in return, is when we are most blessed with gifts of satisfaction and fulfillment.

98. *Help a stranger*

"A stranger is just a friend I haven't met yet."
~Will Rogers

"For I was hungry and you gave Me food; I was thirsty and you gave me drink; I was a stranger and you took Me in; I was naked and you clothed Me; I was sick and you visited Me; I was in prison and you came to Me"
~Matthew 25:35

• *The Lemon:* A stranger in need is…too bad. Apathetic and insensitive to others; friend, foe, or otherwise.

• *Ingredients:* Openness and Open-mindedness – easily approachable and wanting to listen. Compassion, Kindness, Fairness – true concern. Focus – being focused on people you don't yet know requires concentration. Volunteering – many options available. Other-centered – leave your worries on the doorstep. Empathetic altruism – for the good of others with their best interests in mind. Purpose – this may be your journey. Trust – giving the benefit of the doubt and believing in good nature.

• *Preparation:* Make eye contact. Smile. Use body language and positive facial expressions to show that you are easily approachable. Provide a safe environment in which to show and express emotions. Keep them company. Help them remember good times. Don't lecture. Listen. Realize that you don't always need to share your opinion. Learn about grief. The more you know, the more you can help others. Volunteer at a homeless shelter, a food pantry or home for the disabled. Help them realize that reaching out for support is a great first step on the road to success or recovery. Truly appreciate the fact that every little thing that you do can make a big difference in someone else's life. Whatever you do, do it with no thought of reward. People in a hurry are much less likely to help strangers, even if the stranger is a man lying injured on the ground. Also, your mindset determines how likely you are to help. If you are thinking positive and altruistic thoughts, you are more likely to lend a helping hand. Recent estimates that in New York City alone there are over 35,000 homeless individuals who could use some help. Look for opportunities,

• *The Lemonade:* Believing that there are no such things as strangers. Helping people achieve their goals is sometimes more fulfilling than actually achieving your own – unless one of your goals is to help others. Knowing that you made a significant difference in someone's life is beyond gratifying and rewarding. The outcome of these feelings will be better personal and professional relationships, lower stress, and a "helper's high", which in turn, will yield greater career, spiritual, and moral satisfaction. It is empowering and will result in much rejoicing and happiness.

99. What are the odds?

"For a manager to be perceived as a positive manager, they need a four to one positive to negative contact ratio."
~Ken Blanchard

"Below 3 to 1, positivity may well be inert, swamped as it is by the greater potency of negativity. Perhaps only above 3 to 1 do the underdogs of positivity gain adequate strength in numbers to stand up to and overcome negativity. Positivity may need to accumulate and compound to a certain degree before it reaches the crucial tipping point."
~Barbara Fredrickson

• *The Lemon:* Having a positivity to negativity ratio of less than 3:1 is associated with floundering, failing companies, corporations, marriages, and relationships. Twice as much positivity as negativity (2 to 1) is not enough to keep from languishing. If your ratio is below 1 to 1 put down this book and seek professional help.

• *Ingredients:* Mindfulness – attention to your emotional states. Emotional Intelligence – knowing and using your emotions. Positive interactions – they should occur more than three times as often as negative interactions. Negativity – feels more intense (negativity bias). Positivity – occurs more often (positivity offset). Barbara Fredrickson's Positivity Self-Test - do this online (www.PositivityRatio.com) or from her Positivity book; take it often. Study – your routines; emotional highs and lows.

- *Preparation:* Look for ways to increase the positivity in your life (relative to the negativity) and you'll begin to thrive. Pay close attention to your routines, interactions, and daily circumstances to find the events that elicit the most significant emotional responses. After practicing this, identify and delineate what people, things, conversations, situations, and events elevate or depress your mood and feelings. Start making specific changes guided by what you've observed and identified. Improve your ratio by increasing the positives, decreasing the negatives, or doing both. Often it is easier to reduce (not entirely eliminate) negativity than it is to increase positivity. The desire to change and being mindful of what pulls you down or elevates you are the two essential characteristics that you'll need to begin working on your ratio.

- *The Lemonade:* Positive to negative ratios of 3 to 1 to 10 to 1 are associated with flourishing; successful companies, businesses, relationships, and marriages. In addition, a ratio above 3 to 1 is associated with less depressive symptoms and greater remission. A great way to start reaping the multitude of positivity benefits is to work on increasing your positivity ratio. It is the journey to long-lasting happiness.

100. Don't regret

"I have no regrets in my life. I think that everything happens to you for a reason. The hard times that you go through build character, making you a much stronger person." ~Rita Mero

"Regret for the things we did can be tempered by time; it is regret for the things we did not do that is inconsolable." ~Sydney Smith

• *The Lemon:* Saying, "If only..." Having a negative view of past decisions and behaviors. Embarrassment, shame, sadness, or guilt over actions committed or actions not taken. Regrets can anchor you to the past and restrict you from enjoying the present or future.

• *Ingredients:* Forgiveness – allows you to move on. Visualize – your future when you make decisions. Responsibility – blaming won't decrease regret. Conscientiousness - in performing tasks. Curiosity and Courage – doing things that you aren't entirely comfortable with can decrease the chance of regretting inactivity.

• *Preparation:* (1) Avoid regret: On your deathbed, what will you wish you had done? Do it! What will you be glad that you didn't do? Don't do it. When you make decisions, try to visualize yourself in the future. If you're a happy person, assume that you will be happy with either choice. The difference will be what you might regret. Which of the choices is more likely to induce feelings of regret? Should I go to Europe for the summer or stay home. Going to Europe involves extra costs, new experiences and new friends, and spending time with people I don't know. Staying home involves saving money and relaxing with friends and family. They both have a lot of positives; but ten years from now I will probably regret not experiencing Europe and meeting new people more than I will miss relaxing time and saving money. Regret often comes from not doing things we wish we had done. (2) Reduce regret: Ask forgiveness when appropriate, including for yourself. Keep things in perspective. Take responsibility and stop blaming others for what was done or not done. Allow yourself a chance to grieve and then move beyond regret to take advantage of the opportunity to learn and --grow from this. Try to learn something about yourself. Did the regret involve a toxic relationship or your fear of trying something new? Try to change your attitude or behavior to avoid having similar regrets in the future.

• *The Lemonade:* Accountability and responsibility lie beyond regret. Reducing regret or learning how to benefit from it is empowering. It leads to a redemption from the past; allowing you to move on to an amazing present and brighter future. Looking back at your past with fond memories, pride, and a sense of satisfaction.

101. Read these books

- *The Lemon:* Watching TV or mindlessly reading fictional novels that take your time but don't give much in return.

- *Ingredients:* Reading lamp. Books or e-reader. Time. Energy. Effort. Desire, Motivation - to learn and grow, Openness and Curiosity - to what you might find.

- *Preparation:* Take the time to read these books. They will edify, entertain and enlighten.

- *The Lemonade:*

✓ *A Primer in Positive Psychology* by Dr. Christopher Peterson. New York: Oxford University Press, 2006.

✓ *Authentic Happiness* by Dr. Martin Seligman. New York: Free Press, 2002.

✓ *Character Strengths and Virtues* by Dr. Martin Seligman and Dr. Christopher Peterson. New York: Oxford University Press, 2004.

✓ *Chicken Soup for the Soul: 101 Stories to Open the Heart and Rekindle the Spirit* by Jack Canfield and Mark Victor Hansen. Deerfield Beach, FL: Health Communications, 1993.

✓ *Counterclockwise: Mindful Health and the Power of Possibility* by Dr. Ellen Langer. New York: Ballantine Books, 2009.

✓ *First Things First* by Dr. Stephen R. Covey. New York, NY: Simon & Schuster, 1995.

✓ *Flourish* by Dr. Martin Seligman. New York: Free Press, 2011.

✓ *Flow: The Psychology of Optimal Experience* by Dr. Mihaly Csikszentmihalyi. New York: Harper & Row, 1990.

✓ *Forgiveness Is a Choice: A Step-By-Step Process for Resolving Anger and Restoring Hope* by Dr. Robert Enright, American Psychological Association, 2001.

✓ *Full Catastrophe Living: Using the Wisdom of Your Body and Mind to Face Stress, Pain, and Illness* by Dr. Jon Kabat-Zinn. New York: Delta, 1990.

✓ *Happier: Learn the Secrets to Daily Joy and Lasting Fulfillment* by Dr. Tal Ben-Shahar. New York: McGraw-Hill, 2007.

✓ *Happiness and the Human Spirit: The Spirituality of Becoming the Best You Can Be* by Rabbi Dr. Abraham Twerski. Woodstock, VT: Jewish Lights Publishing, 2008.

✓ *Happiness: Unlocking the Mysteries of Psychological Wealth* by Dr. Ed Diener and Robert Biswas-Diener. Malden, MA: Blackwell, 2008.

✓ *Happy for No Reason: 7 Steps to Being Happy from the Inside Out* by Marci Shimoff. New York: Free Press, 2008.

✓ *How Full is Your Bucket* by Tom Rath and Dr. Donald Clifford. New York, NY: Gallup Press, 2004.

✓ *It Wasn't How it Seemed: True stories about people who jumped to conclusions* by Yehudis Samet. Brooklyn, New York: Shaar Press, 2006.

✓ *Lasting Contribution: How to Think, Plan, and Act to Accomplish Meaningful Work* by Dr. Tad Waddington. Chicago, Agape, 2007.

✓ *The Law of the Garbage Truck* by David Pollay, New York: Sterling Publishing, 2010.

✓ *Learned Optimism* by Dr. Martin Seligman. New York: Alfred A. Knopf, 1991.

✓ *Letting Go of the Person You Used to Be: Lessons on Change, Loss, and Spiritual Transformation* by Lama Surya Das. New York: Broadway Books, 2003.

✓ *Mindfulness* by Dr. Ellen Langer. Cambridge, MA: DaCapo Press, 1989.

✓ *Positivity: Groundbreaking Research Reveals How to Embrace the Hidden Strength of Positive Emotions, Overcome Negativity and Thrive* by Dr. Barbara Fredrickson. New York: Crown Publishing, 2009.

✓ *Positive Psychology in Practice* by Alex Linley and Stephen Joseph. Hoboken, New Jersey: Wiley, 2004.

✓ *Steps to REACH forgiveness and to Reconcile* by Dr. EL Worthington, Jr. Boston, MA: Pearson Custom Publishing, 2008.

✓ *Stumbling on Happiness* by Dr. Daniel Gilbert. New York: Vintage Books, 2005.

✓ *Success Principles* by Jack Canfield and Janet Switzer. New York, Harper Paperbacks, 2006.

✓ *Thanks! How the new science of gratitude can make you happier* by Dr. Robert Emmons. New York: Houghton Mifflin Co, 2007.

✓ *The 7 Habits of Highly Effective People* by Dr. Stephen Covey. New York, NY: Free Press, 2004.

✓ *The Art of Happiness: A Handbook for Living* by Dalai Lama and Dr. Howard C. Cutler. New York: Riverhead, 1998.

✓ *The HOW of Happiness: A New Approach to Getting the Life You Want* by Dr. Sonja Lyubomirsky. New York: Penguin Press, 2008.

✓ *The Miracle of Mindfulness: An Introduction to the Practice of Mindfulness* by Thich Nhat Hanh. Boston: Beacon Press, 1987.

✓ *The No Complaining Rule: Positive Ways to Deal with Negativity at Work* by Jon Gordon. Hoboken, New Jersey: Wiley, 2008.

✓ *The Other Side of the Story: Giving people the benefit of the doubt – stories and strategies* by Yehudis Samet. Brooklyn, New York: Mesorah Publications, 2006.

✓ *The Power of Now* by Eckhart Tolle. Novato, CA: New World Library, 1999.

✓ *The Power of Positive Thinking* by Norman Vincent Peale. New York: Fawcett Columbine, 1996

✓ *The Pursuit of Perfect* by Dr. Tal Ben-Shahar. New York: McGraw-Hill, 2009.

✓ *The Secret* by Rhonda Byrne New York: Atria Books, 2006.

✓ *Timeless Wisdom: A Treasury of Universal Truths* by Gary Fenchuk. Midlothian, VA: Cake Eaters, Inc, 1998.

✓ *Train Your Mind, Change Your Brain* by Sharon Begley. New York: Baltimore, 2007.

✓ *Words from the Heart: A Practical Guide to Writing an Ethical Will* by Dr. Eric Weiner. Milwaukee, WI: 2010.

✓ *Words That Hurt, Words That Heal* by Rabbi Joseph Telushkin. New York: Harper, 1996.

Making Lemonade

For more information or to order additional products such as books, seminars/speaking, consulting, please email:

info@dhwi.net

Please visit

Dynamic Health & Wellness Institute:

www.dhwi.net

Dynamic Health & Wellness Institute

About the Author

Neil Farber received his Bachelor of Science degree with Honors in Psychology at Arizona State University and went on to complete doctorates in Pharmacology and Toxicology and a Medical Degree from the Medical College of Wisconsin. Dr. Farber has been inducted into many honor societies and received numerous research and fellowship awards. He is an Associate Professor of Pediatrics, Pharmacology & Toxicology and Anesthesiology and a practicing Pediatric Anesthesiologist at an amazing Children's Hospital. He is a lecturer and researcher in positivity, wellness and mindfulness, conflict management and parenting as well as an expert writer for Psychology Today's Happiness section. Dr. Farber has set up a program called *Creating a Positive Perioperative Environment* to help both patients and healthcare workers. He is a high-ranking Martial Arts Master and enjoys spending time with his beautiful children – all of whom are above average. Dr. Farber is involved in international medical missions in South America, Israel, Asia, Africa and the Philippines to which a portion of the book proceeds are donated.

1956808R00132

Made in the USA
San Bernardino, CA
23 February 2013